THE GEOMETER'S SKETCHPAD®

Reference Manual

Key Curriculum Press
Key College Publishing

The Geometer's Sketchpad®

Dynamic Geometry® Software for Exploring Mathematics
Version 4.0, Fall 2001

Sketchpad Design: Nicholas Jackiw

Software Implementation: Nicholas Jackiw and Scott Steketee

Support: Keith Dean, Jill Binker, Matt Litwin

Reference Manual Authors: Scott Steketee, Nicholas Jackiw, Steven Chanan

Production: Jill Binker, Deborah Cogan, Diana Jean Parks, Caroline Ayres

The Geometer's Sketchpad project began as a collaboration between the Visual Geometry Project at Swarthmore College and Key Curriculum Press. The Visual Geometry Project was directed by Drs. Eugene Klotz and Doris Schattschneider. Portions of this material are based upon work supported by the National Science Foundation under awards to KCP Technologies, Inc. Any opinions, findings, and conclusions or recommendations expressed in this publication are those of the authors and do not necessarily reflect the views of the National Science Foundation.

Key Curriculum Press
1150 65th Street
Emeryville, CA 94608 USA
1-510-595-7000

http://www.keypress.com/sketchpad
techsupport@keypress.com

Printed in the United States of America

10 9 8 7 6 5 4 3 2 1   04 03 02 01

ISBN 1-55953-531-8

Contents

Advanced Topics 213

Index 236

Introduction

The Geometer's Sketchpad is a software system for creating, exploring, and analyzing a wide range of mathematics. Using Dynamic Geometry, you can construct interactive mathematical models ranging from basic investigations about shape and number to advanced, animated illustrations of complex systems. If you're a student, Sketchpad can help you explore not only the topics from your geometry course, but mathematical ideas in algebra, trigonometry, calculus, and other areas. If you're a teacher, Sketchpad provides a compelling environment with which to present mathematical concepts, model classroom questions, and encourage student conjecturing, whether in a hands-on computer lab or on a demonstration screen before an entire class. Researchers and other mathematics enthusiasts use Sketchpad to help pose "what if?" thought experiments, to help probe properties of constructions, and to help discover new results—as well as to create high-quality mathematical illustrations for use in activities and assignments, reports and publications, or simply for their intrinsic visual appeal.

Use the *Learning Guide* that accompanies this *Reference Manual* as your starting point, if you're just beginning to use Sketchpad. That guide contains installation instructions and many guided tours to introduce you to Sketchpad and start you on the path of Dynamic Geometry discovery. This *Reference Manual* contains a definitive description of every Sketchpad tool and command. Consult it after the *Learning Guide* when you want to review a particular software function or when you want to deepen your understanding of how Sketchpad can help you pursue, discover, and enjoy mathematics.

Elements

If you've worked through the *Learning Guide,* you already have a good sense of many of the elements of Sketchpad. Broadly speaking, you use Sketchpad to create documents containing mathematical diagrams and geometric figures. Each diagram or figure—each sketch—is constructed from individual objects that are defined in terms of their mathematical relationships to each other. You use a combination of tools and menu commands to interact with documents and the objects in them. While the next two sections describe each of these tools and commands in detail, this section introduces the various types of objects you'll create and surveys the tools and commands you'll use to manipulate them. Refer to this section when you encounter unfamiliar types of objects in Sketchpad or when you're looking for properties of objects you're already acquainted with.

Documents

A document in Sketchpad contains one or more *sketches*—that is, one or more collections of related mathematical objects. To create these objects, you'll use Sketchpad's Toolbox and menus, described later in this manual.

A document appears on your screen in a window, and can be saved to your computer's hard drive. Once saved, the document can later be reopened from the hard drive.

The document window displays one page at a time.

When a document contains more than a single sketch, each individual sketch is called a *page*. A document can also contain any number of custom tools, which extend the fundamental **Point, Compass,** and **Straightedge** tools in the Toolbox.

Use **Document Options** in the File menu to manage the pages and tools contained in a Sketchpad document.

See also: Document Windows (p. 5), Document Pages (p. 6), Document Tools (p. 7), Document Options (p. 104), Custom Tools (p. 90), An Overview of the Toolbox (p. 69), Menu Reference (p. 101).

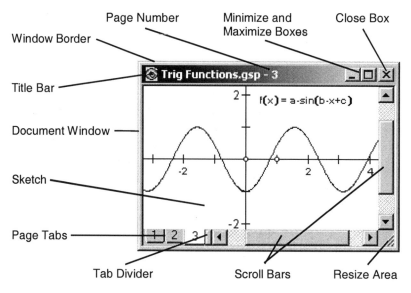

Document Window (Windows)

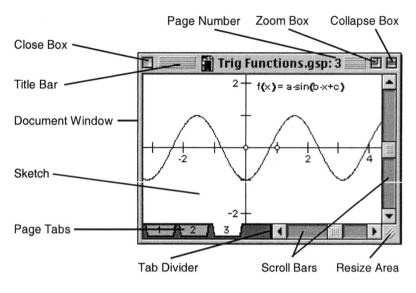

Document Window (Macintosh)

Document Windows

A Sketchpad document window is shown above. The window contains a sketch area within which you construct mathematical figures, and various controls with which you can manipulate the window and the sketch.

Title Bar: Drag to reposition the window on the screen.

Close Box: Click to close the window.

Page Tabs: Click to change pages (only present if your document has more than one page).

Tab Divider: Drag to provide more or less space for page tabs (only present if your document has more than one page).

Because some sketch objects, like lines and rays, extend beyond the normal scrollable area, you can always press a scroll bar's buttons even when the scroll bar itself is at its limit.

Scroll Bars: Click or drag to scroll the window.

Resize Area: Drag to change the window's size.

Several of the controls depend on which type of computer you have.

If you're using a Windows computer:

Window Border: Drag any border of the window to change its size.

Maximize Box: Click to expand the window to the largest possible size.

Minimize Box: Click to shrink the window to an icon.

If you're using a Macintosh:

Zoom Box: Click to expand or contract the window.

Collapse Box: Click to shrink the window to its title bar only.

See also: Document Pages (p. 6), Document Tools (p. 7)

Document Pages

A new Sketchpad document always begins with a single page or sketch—one view of the geometric plane. Over time, you may want to add additional pages to a document. For example, you may want to organize a series of sketches that develop an argument; you may want to present an activity that has several parts; or you may want to explore a conjecture in more depth than would be possible in a single sketch.

In each of these cases, it's convenient to store several sketches together as pages of the same document.

To add pages to a document—and to name, copy, reorder, or remove existing pages—choose **Document Options** from the File menu.

Use **Document Options** to hide or show the page tabs.

When a document has more than one page, page tabs normally appear at the bottom left of the document window, and a page name or number appears in the window's title bar. Click on a page tab to switch from one page of your document to another. You can also create Link buttons to jump between pages.

See also: Document Windows (p. 5), Document Tools (p. 7), Document Options (p. 104), Link Buttons (p. 37)

Document Tools

In addition to multiple pages, a Sketchpad document may contain one or more custom tools—tools that you or someone else has created. Custom tools extend Sketchpad's fundamental tools to provide new mathematical objects or to provide new ways to construct familiar mathematical objects.

Organize custom tools you use frequently by storing each collection of related tools in a document of its own. If you use a document's pages to describe the tools it contains—and give examples of their use—your document becomes a handy "toolkit" that you can share with other people. For example, you might want to make a kit of tools for constructing different centers of a triangle or one for constructing various regular polygons.

When you create a new custom tool, it becomes part of your document. Use **Document Options** to rename, reorder and remove custom tools from the active document, and to copy tools from a different open document into the active document.

When you're working in a sketch, you can use not only the custom tools located in the document on which you're working, but also any custom tools contained in other open documents. To work with custom tools contained in a document on your hard drive, open the document so its custom tools become available. Alternately, if you store any documents in the Tool Folder located on your hard drive next to the Sketchpad application, tools from these documents are available whenever you start Sketchpad—even if the documents that contain them are not open.

See also: Document Windows (p. 5), Document Pages (p. 6), Custom Tools (p. 90), Document Options (p. 104), Tool Folder (p. 98)

Script View of a Tool

You can view the details of a tool in written form, using the Script View. This view shows you a list of each given object and each constructed object of the tool, allows you to modify the tool in various ways, and allows you to watch the tool in detail as it operates. Use the **Show Script View** command in the Custom Tools menu, or the Show Script View checkbox in the Tool Options dialog box, to see the Script View of the active custom tool.

See also: Script View (p. 57), Custom Tools Menu (p. 91), Show Script View (Custom Tools menu) (p. 96), Show Script View (Tool Options dialog) (p. 106)

Objects

From one perspective, mathematics is the art of creating new knowledge by finding new and interesting relationships among existing mathematical objects. Sketchpad provides you with a rich set of such mathematical objects and with many ways of connecting them. It's up to you to create those objects and their connections, and then to investigate their behavior, find new relationships, discover symmetry and patterns, and display and present your results.

The objects you can create in Sketchpad fit into several general categories. Some of the objects are purely geometric entities—points, lines, rays, segments, circles, arcs, interiors, loci, and some iterations. Other objects are either numeric or algebraic entities—measurements, parameters, coordinate systems, calculations, and functions. And finally, some objects in Sketchpad—captions and action buttons—are primarily used in descriptions, explanations, and presentations.

This chapter describes the various kinds of objects with which you can work in Sketchpad. Refer to the Toolbox section (p. 69) for more information on how to use Sketchpad's tools to create and modify objects, and refer to the Menu section (p. 101) for more details on how to use Sketchpad's menus.

See also: Menu Reference (p. 101), Toolbox Reference (p. 69)

Object Attributes

There are several attributes that many or all objects have in common.

Color

Every object in Sketchpad can be colored. To set an object's color, select the object and choose a color from the Color submenu of the Display menu. If an object can have a label, you can set the color for the label as well, using the Text Palette. Some objects, such as measurements and functions, display only text; for such objects you can set the color with either the Color submenu or the Text Palette.

Label

Most geometric objects in Sketchpad can be labeled. To show or hide an object's label, use the **Text** tool or use the **Show/Hide Label** command in the Display menu. To change the label, use the **Text** tool or Label

Properties. To change the font, size, style or color of the label, use the Text Palette.

Visibility

Objects can be hidden from view, although such objects remain present in the sketch and continue to control or influence other objects. Use the **Hide Objects** command in the Display menu to hide an object, and use **Show All Hidden** or Object Properties to show hidden objects. You can also create action buttons to show and hide objects.

Animation

All geometric objects and parameters can be animated so that they move or change of their own accord. Choose **Animate** from the Display menu or create an Animation or Movement action button or use the Motion Controller to start an animation. Movement and Animation action buttons allow you to repeat a desired animation conveniently.

Tracing

Any geometric object can be traced so that as it moves it leaves behind on the screen a trace showing where it's been. Choose **Trace** from the Display menu to trace an object (or to stop tracing an already traced object). Use **Erase Traces** to remove collected traces from the screen and use Color Preferences to determine whether—and how quickly—traces fade from the screen.

Line Width

Many geometric objects are displayed with straight or curved lines. Use the **Line Width** submenu on the Display menu to set the width of such lines or to display dashed lines.

Properties

You can display and change many of the properties of an object using the Object Properties dialog box. Select the object and choose **Properties** from the Edit menu. You can also right-click (Windows) or Ctrl-click (Macintosh) on the object to display a Context menu and choose **Properties** from the Context menu.

See also: Display Menu (p. 143), Color (p. 8), Text Tool (p. 86), Show/Hide Labels (p. 147), Label Properties (p. 122), Text Palette (p. 53), Hide Objects (p. 146), Show All Hidden (p. 146), Animate (p. 150), Animation Buttons (p. 112), Trace (p. 148), Line

Width (p. 143), Properties (p. 120), Context Menu (p. 207), Motion Controller (p. 39), Movement Button (p. 113)

Object Relationships: Parents and Children

Without relationships, this figure could be dragged apart into six disconnected points and six disconnected segments.

When you create a sketch, the sketch includes not just the geometric objects you've constructed, but also the relationships between those objects. When you construct the triangle shown at right, your sketch includes more than just six points and six segments; it also includes the relationships between those 12 objects. For instance, midpoint *E* depends on segment *BC;* when you choose **Midpoint** from the Construct menu you create, not just a point, but also a relationship. Specifically, point *E* is the midpoint of segment *BC*. More generally, we describe that relationship by saying that point *E* is the *child* of segment *BC* and that segment *BC* is the *parent* of point *E*. Similarly, segment *AB* is the child of its two endpoints *A* and *B*, and those endpoints are the parents of segment *AB*.

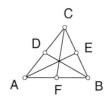

These parent-child relationships define the mathematics of your sketch and are crucial to the way your sketches behave when you explore them by dragging. Object relationships keep the triangle together as a triangle, and relationships make the midpoints stay where they belong when you drag a vertex.

You can think of a sketch as a family tree, defined both by the objects in the sketch and by their parent-child relationships.

These parent and child relationships are implicit in everything you do in Sketchpad. For instance, to use a command from the Construct menu, you must first select certain objects *(prerequisites)* in your sketch. These prerequisites become the parents of the newly constructed child.

To explore an object's mathematical definition—its family tree—use **Select Parents** and **Select Children** from the Edit menu, and use the Parents and Children pop-up menus in Object Properties. You can even rearrange your sketch's family tree using the **Split** and **Merge** commands.

See also: Object Properties (p. 121), Select Parents (p. 115), Select Children (p. 115), Construct Menu (p. 153), Midpoint (p. 154), Arrow Tool (p. 70), Split/Merge (p. 115)

Points

Points are the fundamental building blocks of classical geometry, and geometric figures such as lines and circles are defined in terms of points. All of Sketchpad's geometric constructions begin with points.

Points in Sketchpad are of three kinds.

- An *independent point* has no parents, and so does not depend on any other object. An independent point is free to move anywhere on the sketch plane.

- A *point on path* is constructed on a path object such as a line or circle. A point on path is free to move along its path, but cannot leave that path.

- A *dependent point*—such as a point of intersection—is constructed in such a way that its position is completely determined by its parents. A dependent point cannot move by itself. The point can move only if at least one of its parent objects also moves. Thus, a point at the intersection of two segments cannot move unless one or both of the intersecting segments is moved, and the reflected image of a point cannot move unless either the pre-image or the mirror moves.

See also: Object Relationships: Parents and Children (p. 9), Point Tool (p. 80), Straightedge Tools (p. 83), Compass Tool (p. 81), Custom Tools (p. 90), Path Objects (p. 13)

Moving and Animating Points

Independent points and points on paths can be dragged and animated (using either **Animate** from the Display menu or using an Animation button), and they can be moved with Movement buttons. When you move or animate any other geometric object, it moves by moving the parents on which the object depends.

See also: Animate (p. 150), Animation Buttons (p. 36), Animation Button (p. 112) Movement Button (p. 113), Object Relationships: Parents and Children (p. 9)

Splitting and Merging Points

There may be times when you want to attach an independent point to another object or make a point that has parents independent of those parents. The **Split** and **Merge** commands in the Edit menu allow you to make these changes in the family tree of your sketch.

Transformed and plotted points cannot be split.

Use **Split** to separate any point on a path, midpoint, or intersection from its parents, making it into an independent point.

Use **Merge** to merge an independent point with any other point or with a path.

See also: Split/Merge (p. 115), Object Relationships: Parents and Children (p. 9)

Constructing Points

There are many different ways to construct points in a sketch.

You can also construct a point by using commands from the Transform menu to create a transformed image of an existing point.

- Click the **Point** tool to construct a point.

- Click the **Straightedge** tool or the **Compass** tool in empty space to construct a point that determines a straight object or circle. Many **Custom** tools can also construct points as you use them.

- Choose **Point On Object** to construct a point on each selected path object.

- Choose **Midpoint** to construct a midpoint on each selected segment.

- Choose **Intersection** to construct the intersection point of two selected objects. Each object must be a straight object, a circle, or an arc.

- Choose the **Plot Points** command to plot a point with coordinates defined by two selected measurements or by two numbers you specify.

See also: Point Tool (p. 80), Straightedge Tools (p. 83), Compass Tool (p. 81), Custom Tools (p. 90), Path Objects (p. 13), Point On Object (p. 153), Midpoint (p. 154), Intersection (p. 155), Plot Points (p. 201)

Using Points in Transformations

You can transform points using the Transform menu. You can also use points in a number of different ways to help specify how other objects will be transformed.

- Use **Mark Center** to designate a center point for rotation and dilation.

- Use **Mark Angle** to designate the angle formed by three points for translation and rotation.

- Use **Mark Ratio** to designate the ratio formed by three collinear points for dilation.

See also: Transform Menu (p. 164), Mark Center (p. 166), Mark Angle (p. 166), Mark Ratio (p. 167)

Measuring Points

Several of the Measure menu's commands apply to selected points or to combinations of points.

- Use **Distance** to measure the distance between two points.

- Use **Angle** to measure the angle formed by three points.

- Use **Ratio** to measure the ratio defined by three collinear points.

- Use **Abscissa** to measure the *x*-coordinate of a point.

- Use **Ordinate** to measure the *y*-coordinate of a point.

- Use **Coordinates** to measure the coordinates of a point.

See also: Angle (p. 189), Ratio (p. 192), Abscissa (p. 195), Ordinate (p. 195), Coordinates (p. 194)

Path Objects

There are certain geometric objects in Sketchpad on which you can construct and animate points. These objects are collectively referred to as *path objects*. Path objects include:

- straight objects (segments, rays, lines, and axes)

- circles and arcs

For polygons and other interiors, the perimeter of the interior forms that interior's path.

- polygons and other interiors

- point loci and function plots

You can use the **Point On Object** command to construct a point on any path object.

See also: Segments, Rays, and Lines (p. 14), Circles and Arcs (p. 15), Polygons and Other Interiors (p. 16), Loci (p. 23), Point On Object (p. 153), Animate (p. 150), Animation (p. 42)

Segments, Rays, and Lines

Segments, rays, and lines are fundamental objects in Euclidean geometry. In classical geometric constructions, a straightedge is used to construct these objects.

Constructing Straight Objects

Sketchpad provides several different ways to construct straight objects..

- Use the **Straightedge** tool to construct a straight object using two points.

- Use the **Segment, Ray,** or **Line** command to construct a straight object using two selected points.

- Use the **Perpendicular Line** or **Parallel Line** command to construct a line parallel or perpendicular to a selected straight object.

- Use the **Angle Bisector** command to construct the ray bisecting the angle formed by three selected points.

Using Straight Objects

- Use a straight object as a path along which to animate a point by creating the point with the **Point On Object** command.

- Use a straight object as a path along which to animate an independent point by using the **Merge** command.

- Use a straight object as a mirror for reflections by choosing the **Mark Mirror** command.

- Construct a segment's **Midpoint.**

- Construct a straight object's **Intersection** with any other straight object, circle, or arc.

- Use **Define Unit Distance** to define a coordinate system with a unit distance defined by one or two selected segments. (The unit of the coordinate system is defined by the length of the segment.)

If you use two selected segments, the first defines the unit for *x,* and the second for *y.*

Measuring Straight Objects

You can measure:

- the **Length** of a segment.

- the **Ratio** of two segments' lengths.

- the **Equation** of a line.

- the **Slope** of any straight object.

See also: Straightedge Tools (p. 83), Segment (p. 83), Ray (p. 83), Line (p. 83), Perpendicular Line (p. 157), Parallel Line (p. 156), Angle Bisector (p. 158), Mark Mirror (p. 166), Point On Object (p. 153), Split/Merge (p. 115), Midpoint (p. 154), Intersection (p. 155), Length (p. 188), Ratio (p. 192), Equation (p. 196), Slope (p. 196)

Circles and Arcs

Circles and arcs are fundamental objects in Euclidean geometry. In classical geometric constructions, a compass is used to construct these objects.

Constructing Circles

Sketchpad provides several different ways to construct a circle.

- Use the **Compass** tool to construct a circle using a center point and another point which defines the radius.

- Use the **Circle By Center+Point** command to construct a circle using a center point and another point which defines the radius.

- Use the **Circle By Center+Radius** command to construct a circle using a center point and either a segment or a distance measurement to define the radius.

Constructing Arcs

- Use the **Arc Through 3 Points** command to construct an arc which passes through three selected points.

- Use the **Arc On Circle** command to construct an arc which lies on a selected circle and is bounded by two selected points on the circle.

Using Circles and Arcs

- Use a circle or an arc as a path along which to animate a point by creating the point with the **Point On Object** command.

- Use a circle or an arc as a path along which to animate an existing point by using the **Merge** command.

- Construct the **Interior** of a circle or the **Arc Segment** or **Arc Sector** interior of an arc.

- Construct the **Intersection** of a circle or an arc with a straight object, a circle, or an arc.

- Use **Define Unit Circle** to define a coordinate system that uses the selected circle as its unit circle.

Measuring Circles and Arcs

You can measure:

- the **Circumference** of a circle.

- the **Radius** of a circle or an arc.

- the **Area** of a circle.

- the **Equation** of a circle.

- the **Arc Length** of an arc.

- the **Arc Angle** of an arc.

See also: Compass Tool (p. 81), Circle By Center+Point (p. 158), Circle By Center+Radius (p. 159), Arc Through 3 Points (p. 160), Arc On Circle (p. 160), Point On Object (p. 153), Split/Merge (p. 115), Interior (p. 161), Intersection (p. 155), Define Unit Circle (p. 197), Circumference (p. 189), Radius (p. 192), Area (p. 190), Equation (p. 196), Arc Length (p. 192), Arc Angle (p. 191)

Polygons and Other Interiors

There are four kinds of objects in Sketchpad that define a region of a plane. These include polygons, circle interiors, and two kinds of arc interiors: arc sectors and arc segments.

Constructing Interiors

- Use **Polygon Interior** to construct a polygon defined by three or more selected vertex points.

- Use **Circle Interior** to construct the interior of each selected circle.

- Use **Interior | Arc Sector** to construct the sector interior of each selected arc. An arc sector is bounded by the arc and by the radii to the two endpoints of the arc.

- Use **Interior | Arc Segment** to construct the segment interior of each selected arc. An arc segment is bounded by the arc and by the chord connecting the endpoints of the arc.

Using Interiors

- Use an interior as a path along which to animate a point by creating the point with the **Point On Object** command. Such a point travels the perimeter (or circumference) of the interior.

- Use an interior as a path along which to animate an independent point by using the **Merge** command.

Measuring Interiors

You can measure:

- the **Area** of any interior.

- the **Perimeter** of a polygon interior or an arc interior.

- the **Circumference** of a circle interior.

- the **Radius** of a circle interior or an arc interior.

- the **Arc Angle** or **Arc Length** of an arc interior.

See also: Interior (p. 161), Point On Object (p. 153), Merge (p. 115), Area (p. 190), Perimeter (p. 189), Circumference (p. 189), Radius (p. 192), Arc Angle (p. 191), Arc Length (p. 192)

Measurements, Calculations, and Parameters

Numeric values can be used to control transformed objects, plotted points, calculations, functions, and iterations.

Measurements, calculations, and parameters are the three kinds of Sketchpad objects that display numeric values and so have many common characteristics. The numeric values generated by measurements—and by calculations based on measurements—can be observed in order to discover relationships among objects in your sketch. And the numeric values of all three kinds of objects can be used to define or control the behavior of your sketch in powerful and revealing ways.

Measurements

m $\overline{AB}$ = 2.00 cm

m∠ABC = 35°

Measurements quantify the size, orientation, coordinates, and other characteristics of Sketchpad objects. All measured values update dynamically in Sketchpad when you change the objects they measure. Often you can gain important mathematical insights by observing how measurements change and how they relate to each other and to other objects in the sketch.

All measurements have numeric values of one sort or another. Most measurements (all except for coordinate pair and equation measurements) have a single value; these single-valued measurements can be used for many purposes in your sketch.

To create new measurements, first select objects to measure, then choose a command from the Measure menu.

See also: Measure Menu (p. 187), Using Values (p. 20)

Calculations

2·AB = 4.00 cm

Calculations are mathematical expressions that relate one or more terms—such as measurement—by arithmetic. For example, where each of the interior angles of a triangle may be measured by an angle measurement, the sum of these three angles may be calculated by a calculation. As you change the measurements on which a calculation depends, the calculated result changes accordingly.

Use calculations to gain valuable insights into mathematical relationships or to control sketch objects that you create based on your calculations. To perform a calculation, choose the **Calculate** command. You can define the calculation to use a number of different mathematical operators, built-in functions, and even functions that you've defined yourself.

The Geometer's Sketchpad Reference Manual

- To create a calculation, choose the **Calculate** command.

- To edit an existing calculation, double-click it with the **Arrow** tool, or choose the **Edit Calculation** command.

- To change a calculation into a parameter, edit the calculation so that it includes only a single numeric value and uses no operators or functions. It can have no units, or it can have angle or distance units.

See also: Calculate (p. 194), Calculator (p. 47), Edit Calculation (p. 119), Using Values (p. 20), Functions (p. 27)

Parameters

$t_1 = 1.00$

$t_2 = 1°$

$t_3 = 1.00$ cm

Parameters are simple given numeric values. Unlike measurements and calculations, they do not depend on other objects for their value. A parameter is defined by a single number and an optional unit. Values with degrees or radian units define an angle parameter; values with cm, pixel, or inch units define a length parameter; and values with no units define a scalar parameter. Once defined, parameter values can easily be changed by typing new values or by animating the parameter so that it changes value gradually over some numeric domain.

Use parameters to define mathematical constructions when you want to explore the effects on the construction of varying a numeric quantity.

- To create a parameter, choose the **New Parameter** command or choose New Parameter from within the Calculator.

- To change the value of a parameter, double-click it with the **Arrow** tool or use the Value Properties panel.

- To change the domain, speed or other aspects of how a parameter is animated, use the Parameter Properties panel.

- To increase of decrease the value of a parameter, select it and press the + or − key on your keyboard.

- To animate a parameter, select it and choose the **Animate** command or click the Animate button of the Motion Controller.

- To animate a parameter with an action button, select it and choose **Animation** from the Action Buttons menu.

- To make a parameter depend on some other value in your sketch, choose the **Edit Parameter** command and use the Calculator to redefine the parameter as a calculation, based on other values.

See also: New Parameter (p. 202), Edit Parameter Definition (p. 119), Value Properties (p. 123), Parameter Properties (p. 125), Using Values (p. 20), Calculator (p. 47), Animate (p. 150), Animation Buttons (p. 36) The Motion Controller (p. 39), Animation Button (p. 112), Keyboard Reference (p. 209)

Using Values

All calculations, all parameters, and most measurements have a single numeric value. The values of any of these objects can be used in the same ways.

- Change the value's precision using the Value Properties panel.

You can also use Unit Preferences to set the precision for all new measurements, calculations, and parameters.

- Change the distance units or angle units of this value (and of all values in the sketch) using Unit Preferences.

- Change how the value is labeled using the Value Properties and Label Properties panels.

- Include the value in a calculation or function by clicking the object while using the Calculator.

- Choose **Mark Distance** to use a distance value as the marked distance for translation.

- Choose **Mark Angle** to use an angle value as the marked angle for translation and rotation.

- Choose **Mark Scale Factor** to use a value with no units as the marked scale factor for dilation.

- Choose **Define Unit Distance** to use a distance value as the unit distance for a new coordinate system.

- Select two values and choose **Plot as (x, y)** to plot a point with coordinates given by the selected values.

- Use **Iterate To Depth** to define the depth of an iteration by a selected value.

See also: Value Properties (p. 123), Label Properties (p. 122), Units Preferences (p. 135), Calculate (p. 194), New Function (p. 202), Calculator (p. 47), Mark Distance (p. 170), Mark Angle (p. 166), Mark Scale Factor (p. 168), Define Unit Distance (p. 197), Plot as (x, y) (p. 201), Iterate (p. 178), Parametric Depth (p. 185)

Coordinate Systems and Axes

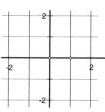

A coordinate system quantizes the plane and the location of objects on it. A coordinate system is defined by an origin, a scale, and a grid form or shape. The origin of a coordinate system is the point or the position at the center of the coordinate axes. The scale of a coordinate system determines the size of each unit on an axis. The grid form of a coordinate system determines how coordinates are measured. In the most common form—a square coordinate system—coordinates are indicated as horizontal and vertical distances from the origin, measured in the same unit scale. Rectangular coordinate systems are like square coordinate systems in that they measure coordinates horizontally and vertically from the origin, but they have separate scales for each axis. Finally, a polar coordinate system measures coordinates by a distance and a direction from the positive horizontal axis, rather than by horizontal and vertical distance from the origin.

The default coordinate system has an origin point in the center of your screen and a unit point at (1, 0). Drag the origin to relocate the coordinate system and drag the unit point to change its scale.

Many of Sketchpad's analytic measurements—such as **Coordinates, Equation,** and **Slope**—and all of the plotting commands—such as **Plot Points, Plot as (x, y),** or **Plot New Function**—are defined in reference to a coordinate system. If you do not create a new coordinate system before using these commands, they will create a default square coordinate system for you, and their results will be defined in terms of that coordinate system.

To create a coordinate system:

- Choose **Define Coordinate System** from the Graph menu. Depending on the objects you've selected, there are several different ways this command constructs the coordinate system.

- Measure or plot a quantity that requires a coordinate system, such as **Coordinates, Coordinate Distance, Slope, Equation,** or **Plot Points.** If you don't already have a coordinate system, any of these commands will create one.

See also: Graph Menu (p. 197), Define Coordinate System (p. 197), Coordinates (p. 194), Abscissa (p. 195), Ordinate (p. 195), Coordinate Distance (p. 195), Slope (p. 196), Equation (p. 196)

Modifying a Coordinate System

Depending on how the coordinate system was defined, some of the Grid Form commands may not be available.

- To change the form of the grid, choose **Polar Grid, Square Grid,** or **Rectangular Grid.** The grid form determines whether the **Coordinates** command measures polar or rectangular coordinates and determines whether the command to plot measured values is **Plot as (x, y)** or **Plot as (r, theta).**

- To hide or show the grid lines, choose **Hide Grid** or **Show Grid.**

- To change the appearance of the grid lines or dots, select the grid by clicking on a grid intersection, then choose **Dotted, Thin,** or **Thick** from the Line Width submenu.

- To change the color of the grid lines, select the grid by clicking on a grid intersection, then choose a color from the Color submenu.

- To make points snap to integer coordinate positions when dragged, choose **Snap Points.**

See also: Graph Menu (p. 197), Grid Form (p. 199), Coordinates (p. 194), Plot as (x, y) (p. 201), Show Grid (p. 200), Line Width (p. 143), Color (p. 144), Snap Points (p. 200), Define Coordinate System (p. 197)

Using a Coordinate System

The scale of a coordinate system may be defined by an object in the sketch; such a coordinate system doesn't have a unit point and cannot be scaled by dragging axis tick-mark labels.

- To change the scale of a coordinate system, drag the unit point. Square coordinate systems have one unit point, and rectangular coordinate systems have two.

- To change the scale of a coordinate system, press and drag any axis tick-mark label with the **Arrow** tool.

- If you have more than one coordinate system, make one of them the active one by choosing **Mark Coordinate System.**

- To plot a point on the coordinate system, choose **Plot Points.**

- To plot two measured values on the coordinate system, select them and choose **Plot as (x, y).**

- To plot a new function on the coordinate system, choose **Plot New Function.**

- To plot an existing function on the coordinate system, select the function and choose **Plot Function.**

See also: Graph Menu (p. 197), Mark Coordinate System (p. 199), Plot Points (p. 201), Plot as (x, y) (p. 201), Plot New Function (p. 203), Functions (p. 27)

Multiple Coordinate Systems

While many sketches require at most one coordinate system, you can create more than one coordinate system if you wish. You might want more than one coordinate system to compare objects—the coordinates of a point or the plot of a function—in the two systems.

When you have more than one coordinate system, only one of those systems is the *marked* or active coordinate system. The marked coordinate system is the one that's used for plotting points and functions and for measurements such as coordinates or slope that require a coordinate system. To change which coordinate system is marked in your sketch:

1. Select the coordinate system you wish to mark by clicking at a grid intersection or on its origin, unit point, or either axis.

2. Choose **Mark Coordinate System** from the Graph menu.

See also: Mark Coordinate System (p. 199), Plot Points (p. 201), Plot as (x, y) (p. 201), Plot New Function (p. 203)

How To . . . Construct a Geoboard

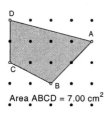

Area ABCD = 7.00 cm²

You can use a coordinate system to make a Sketchpad geoboard. Straight objects you construct on this geoboard will always stick to the grid dots, just like rubber bands attached to the posts on a physical geoboard. And with a Sketchpad geoboard you can construct polygons, measure slopes of lines, measure perimeters and areas of polygons, and "measure" coordinates of points.

1. Choose **Preferences** from the Edit menu and click on the Units tab.

2. Set the Distance units to cm and click OK to close the dialog box.

3. Choose **Define Coordinate System** from the Graph menu.

4. Choose **Display | Line Width | Dotted** to show dots at the grid intersections.

5. Hide the origin, unit point, and axes.

6. Choose **Graph | Snap Points** to make points snap to your geoboard's grid intersections.

Your geoboard is ready for use.

Loci

In geometry, a locus is the set of all possible positions of an object that satisfy some specific condition. For example, you might investigate the locus of points equidistant from two fixed points or the locus of circles that have their center point on a fixed circle and which pass through a fixed point.

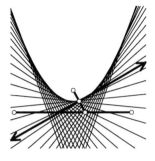

Possible paths include straight objects, circles, arcs, polygons, other interiors, and point loci themselves.

In Sketchpad, a locus describes the position of an object while some point (on which the object depends) travels along a path. More formally, a Sketchpad locus is the set of positions of a *driven object* generated as some *driver point* on which the object depends moves to a finite number of positions along a *drive path*.

A few examples may help: In the first pair of illustrations, point *E* is the midpoint of segment *CD*. The illustration at right shows the locus of point *E* as point *C* travels along segment *AB*. The locus of point *E* forms a smaller segment, parallel to and half the length of segment *AB*. In this example, point *E* is the driven object, point *C* is the driver point, and segment *AB* is the drive path. In the next pair of illustrations, circle *CB* is constructed with points *C* and *B* defined on circle *AB*. The locus of circle *CB* as point *C* travels along circle *AB* is the cardiod shown at right. In this example, circle *CB* is the driven object, point *C* is the driver point, and circle *AB* is the drive path.

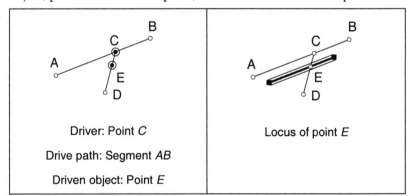

Driver: Point *C*

Drive path: Segment *AB*

Driven object: Point *E*

Locus of point *E*

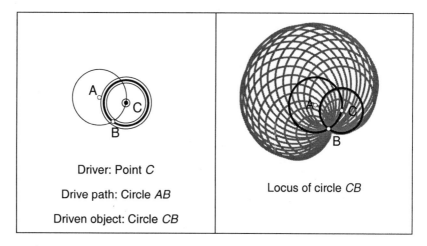

Driver: Point *C*

Drive path: Circle *AB*

Driven object: Circle *CB*

Locus of circle *CB*

If you don't find the terms *driver, drive path,* and *driven object* helpful in understanding the objects that define a locus, consider using other analogies. Some people prefer to think of a Sketchpad locus as a visualization of an abstract function. In this analogy, an independent variable (the driver) is defined over a particular domain (the drive path). The value of that independent variable (that is, the position of the driver on the drive path) determines the value of some dependent variable (that is, the position of the driven object). Each sample of the locus represents one value of the function, and the entire locus is an approximation of the range of the function. (It's an approximation because Sketchpad uses only a finite number of ordered pairs—or samples—in constructing the locus.) The abstract function in this analogy is actually the construction by which the driven object relates to the driver.

Others prefer to think of a Sketchpad locus as a more durable form of a traced animation. In that case, you have an *animating point* (the driver) moving along the *path* on which it's constructed (the drive path) that defines some *traced object* (the driven object). As the animating point moves along its path, the traced object traces out the locus.

The difficulty of naming these dynamic concepts has a long history: When Johan De Witt and Sir Isaac Newton studied locus constructions of the conics in the 17th century, they used the term *directrix* to refer to what we call the driver. Today, when discussing the same type of locus, mathematicians use *directrix* to refer to the drive path instead!

Objects

Using **Plot Properties,** you can set the number of samples Sketchpad uses when calculating and displaying a locus.

Mathematically, a locus may describe an infinite number of positions of the driven object. However, to display an infinite number of positions would require a computer to use an infinite amount of time, so Sketchpad instead displays a large (but not infinite) number of possible positions, rather than *all* possible positions. Each position that Sketchpad does display is called a *sample*.

See also: Locus (p. 163), Animate (p. 150), Trace (p. 148), Path Objects (p. 13)

Constructing a Locus

To construct a locus, you must first construct the driven object—the object whose locus you want to construct— in such a way that it depends on the driver. Either the driver must be a point on path or you must construct a separate path along which to move the driver.

1. Select the driver and the driven object.
2. If the driver is an independent point, select the drive path—a path object that does not depend on the driver.
3. Choose **Locus** from the Construct menu.

See also: Locus (p. 163), Construct Menu (p. 153), Path Objects (p. 13)

Modifying a Locus

You can change the color and line width of a locus just as you do with other objects, and you can show the label of a point locus. There also are some special modifications you can make which apply only to loci.

When a locus is first constructed, the number of samples it uses is determined by a value on the Sampling Preferences panel of **Advanced Preferences**.

Determining the Number of Samples

After a locus has been constructed, you can use the Plot Properties panel of **Properties** to change the number of samples. In general, the higher the number of samples, the better the quality of the locus, but the slower it is to drag.

A point locus is simply the locus of a point, as opposed to the locus of a circle or line or other object.

Continuous and Discrete Point Loci

If the locus is a point locus, you can use the Plot Properties panel of **Properties** to determine whether the locus is displayed in continuous form (with the samples connected to each other) or in discrete form (with a separate dot for each sample).

Resizing a Point Locus

If a point locus is based on a closed path (such as a circle) or a finite path (such as a segment or arc), the domain of the driver is fixed. But if the drive path is infinite and open (such as a ray or line), the domain of the driver—and therefore, the potential size of the locus—is infinite! If possible, Sketchpad limits the domain based on the portion of the path that is visible on the screen. Such a point locus (on an infinite open domain) displays an arrowhead on the end of the locus.

If you wish to change the displayed size of a point locus, use the **Arrow** tool to drag the arrowhead at either end of the locus. Drag in the direction that the arrowhead points to increase the size of the locus; drag in the opposite direction to decrease the size of the locus.

See also: Color (p. 144), Line Width (p. 143), Show/Hide Labels (p. 147), Advanced Preferences (p. 138), Sampling Preferences (p. 139), Properties (p. 120), Plot Properties (p. 124), Resizing Function Plots and Loci (p. 79), Arrow Tool (p. 70)

Functions and Function Plots

Sketchpad allows you to define functions by their equation and to plot them on a coordinate system. Throughout Sketchpad and this manual, the term *function* refers to a symbolic definition, such as $f(x) = 2x$, and the term *function plot* refers to the graph of a function on a specific coordinate system.

See also: Coordinate Systems and Axes (p. 21)

Functions

$$f(x) = a \cdot x^2 + b \cdot x + c$$

Sketchpad allows you to create functions and families of functions, to evaluate functions and use them in calculations, to edit functions, to plot functions and their inverses using either rectangular or polar coordinates, to combine and compose functions in various ways, and to differentiate functions.

Creating a New Function

To create a new function, for example, $f(x) = \sin(x)$, use **New Function.** This command opens Sketchpad's function calculator to allow you to define how the function is calculated.

To create a new function and plot it immediately, use the **Plot New Function** command.

See also: New Function (p. 202), Plot New Function (p. 203), Calculator (p. 47)

Families of Functions

Parameters are particularly useful for investigating families of functions because they can easily be changed or animated.

While you're using the function calculator to enter or edit a function, you can create a new parameter or use an existing parameter or other measurement from your sketch. When the value of this parameter or measurement changes, the definition of the function changes. For example, if you create parameter a while you're specifying the function $f(x) = a \cdot \sin(x)$, you can investigate the behavior and plots of this entire family of functions, including functions such as $f(x) = -1 \cdot \sin(x)$ and $f(x) = 3 \cdot \sin(x)$ by varying the parameter a. Similarly, you can use three parameters as you define the function $f(x) = ax^2 + bx + c$ to investigate the effect on this family of functions of changing each parameter's value.

With the Calculator open add a new parameter to the function definition by choosing **New Parameter** from the Calculator's Values pop-up menu. Insert an existing parameter by clicking on it in the sketch.

See also: New Function (p. 202), Plot New Function (p. 203), Edit Parameter Definition (p. 119), New Parameter (p. 202), Parameters (p. 19), Calculator (p. 47)

Evaluating and Using Functions

Functions can be thought of as rules for turning input values into output values. For example, the function $f(x) = 2 \cdot x + 3$ can be thought of as the rule which says "To get an output value, take the input value, multiply it by 2, then add 3 to the result." Evaluating a function means following the rule for a particular value. For example, $f(5) = 2(5) + 3 = 13$.

$$f(x) = 2 \cdot x + 3$$
$$f(5) = 13.00$$

When using the Calculator, you can click any function visible in your sketch to insert it into the calculation—or new function—that you're defining in the Calculator.

Once you've defined a function, you can use it in later calculations and in later function definitions. The Function pop-up menu in the Calculator includes every selected user-defined function in your sketch. To insert a user-defined function that isn't in the list, click the function in the sketch. (If the Calculator is hiding the function, you may have to move the Calculator out of the way first.) You can choose any of these user-defined functions in the definition of the new calculation or function.

See also: New Function (p. 202), Calculate (p. 194)

Plotting a Function

To define a new function and plot it immediately on the marked coordinate system, choose **Plot New Function.** Define the function as described above. When you close the function calculator, the function is plotted in the form that was set in the function calculator's Equation pop-up menu when you defined the function. The plot can take any of four possible forms.

You can use the $x = f(y)$ form to plot the inverse of a function $y = f(x)$.

- $y = f(x)$

- $x = f(y)$

- $r = f(\theta)$

- $\theta = f(r)$

To plot one or more existing functions on the marked coordinate system, select every function you want to plot and choose **Plot Function.** Each function is plotted in the form that you set in the function calculator's Equation pop-up menu at the time you defined that function.

See also: Plot New Function (p. 203), Function Plots (p. 27)

Editing Functions

You can edit an existing function to change its definition or how it's plotted. Editing a function is useful, for example, if you've plotted the graph of $y = 2 \cdot \sin(x)$, and you want to change the function to $y = 3 \cdot \sin(x)$ in order to see how the two graphs differ. Instead of changing the constant to 3, you can insert a new parameter, allowing you to investigate the plots of the family of functions $y = a \cdot \sin(x)$.

To edit a function, select that function and choose **Edit Function** from the Edit menu or from the Context menu.

Choose a new Equation form while editing a function to change how that function is plotted. For instance, to plot a function *f* as a polar function, change *f*'s Equation form from $y = f(x)$ to $r = f(\theta)$.

When you edit a function, you can redefine it in any way you want—introducing new parameters and existing parameters, measurements and calculations—provided you don't create a circular definition. A circular definition is one that uses a calculation that depends on the function you're editing. For instance, if you've defined a function *f* and used it to calculate $f(3)$ in your sketch, you cannot later edit function *f* so that it uses the calculation of $f(3)$ in its definition.

See also: Edit Function (p. 119), Calculator (p. 47)

Transforming Functions

Once you've defined a function $f(x)$—for example, $f(x) = x^2$— you can define and plot other functions that are transformations of $f(x)$. Transformations of $f(x)$ include such functions as $g(x) = 2 \cdot f(x)$, $g(x) = f(-x)$, or even $g(x) = -3 \cdot f(2x + 5) - 1$.

To define a function that is a transformation of $f(x)$, choose **New Function** from the Graph menu. Define the new function as you normally would, inserting the original function f wherever you want by choosing it from the user-defined section of the Calculator's Function pop-up menu.

See also: New Function (p. 202)

Composite Functions

Composite functions are functions of functions. For instance, $f(g(3))$ is the composition of functions f and g evaluated at 3 and can be thought of as follows: "First evaluate function g at 3. Then use this result as the input for function f. The result of evaluating f is the value of the expression $f(g(3))$."

$$f(x) = 2 \cdot x + 3$$
$$g(x) = x^2$$
$$f(g(3)) = 21.00$$

To compose two functions f and g, you must first define each of the functions separately. Then you can evaluate the composite function (as in the example) or define a new function that is the composite of the two original functions.

To evaluate $f(g(3))$ as in the example, select functions f and g and choose the **Calculate** command. In the Calculator, choose $f(x)$ from the user-defined section of the Function pop-up menu, then choose $g(x)$ similarly. And finally, enter the argument ("3" in this example), close the parentheses, and click OK.

To create the composite function $h(x) = f(g(x))$, choose the **New Function** command to define function $h(x)$, and follow the same process, using x rather than 3 as the argument.

See also: Calculate (p. 194), New Function (p. 202)

Differentiation

To create the derivative of a function with respect to its independent variable, select the function, then choose **Derivative** from the Graph menu. The result is a derivative function that can be plotted or evaluated like any other function.

See also: Derivative (p. 203)

Function Plots

To plot a new function, choose the **Plot New Function** command and use the function calculator to define your function. While you're defining the function, use the Equation pop-up menu to define the form of the plot. (Sketchpad supports several Cartesian and polar equation forms.) When you close the function calculator, both the function and its plot appear.

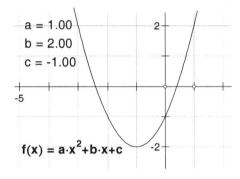

To plot one or more existing functions on the marked coordinate system, select every function you want to plot and choose **Plot Function**. Each function is plotted in the form that was set in the function calculator's Equation pop-up menu at the time you defined that function.

See also: Functions (p. 27), Plot New Function (p. 203), Coordinate Systems and Axes (p. 21)

Iterations and Iterated Images

To *iterate* an action or an operation is to repeat it some number of times. Mathematically, iteration refers to the process of repeatedly applying some mathematical construction, calculation, or other operation to the previous result of that same operation. The operation must define an output in terms of some input, and the iteration uses the output of one step as the input for the next step.

Sketchpad allows you to iterate any of the mathematical relationships you use to construct relationships in a sketch. You can use iterations to create repeated transformations (such as tessellations), to produce fractals and other self-similar objects, or to generate other sequences and series.

In algebra, an iteration is the repetition of a calculation that uses an input value to calculate an output value. The iteration repeatedly applies the calculation to the value that resulted from the previous calculation—the output from one step is the input for the next. To begin the process, there must be a starting value; this value is called the *seed.* Consider the calculation "add 2" applied to the seed 5. When you apply this operation once to 5, the result is 7 (because 5 + 2 = 7). When you then apply the rule to the first result (7), the second result is 9 (because 7 + 2 = 9). Iterating this operation produces the sequence of values 7, 9, 11, 13, 15, 17, ...

In geometry, an iteration uses an operation performed on a set of geometric objects that produces a new set of objects. The original set of objects is the input, and the new set is the output. To begin the process, there must be a starting set of objects; these starting objects are the *pre-image.* Consider the transformation "translate to the right by 1 cm." If you apply this transformation to an initial pre-image Δ*ABC,* the first image result is Δ*A'B'C',* translated 1 cm to the right. Iterating this transformation produces a sequence of triangles congruent to the initial pre-image Δ*ABC,* each shifted 1 cm to the right of the previous triangle in the sequence.

In these examples, it's helpful to think of the operation—"add 2" or "translate to the right by 1 cm"—as distinct from any individual value or triangle in the sequence; rather, think of it as mapping each value or image in the sequence to the next value or image in the sequence. Thus, one might say that 47 maps to 49 under the operation "add 2." The entire iteration is defined by the pre-image (the seed) and the mapping operation. When you apply the operation to the pre-image once, the result is the *first image* of your pre-image according to your mapping operation. As you iterate the operation, you generate the second, third, and fourth images, and so on.

Creating Iterations

Any parameter used to define an iteration must have geometric children.

Iterated operations and constructions in Sketchpad are always created by example, and are always defined in terms of points and parameters. Use the tools and menus to construct a figure in which a set of independent points or parameters is used to produce (through whatever mathematical relationships you wish) an equal number of dependent objects (points or calculated values). The independent objects represent the pre-images or seeds of your iteration; and the corresponding dependent objects represent the first iterated images of those initial objects. Then use **Iterate** in the Transform menu to indicate the correspondence between pre-images and images. The Iterate dialog box allows you to specify the number of times you wish to iterate the construction. The result is a collection of *iterated images* of the pre-images and of every object that depends on the pre-images.

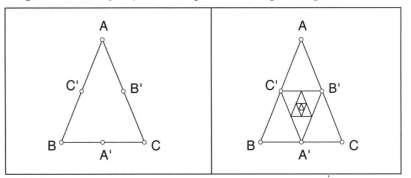

More generally, if a geometric point pre-image A is used to construct a dependent point A', then the iterated image of that point—or the *orbit* of that point's iteration—is the sequence of points A', A'', A''', and so forth.

In the illustration on the left, $\triangle ABC$ and its midpoints $A'B'C'$ have been constructed. In the illustration on the right, the independent vertices of the triangle have been *mapped* to their midpoint images using the Iterate dialog box, and the constructed relationship has been iterated four times. The result is a series of images of the segments and points that defined the initial construction as the triangle is iterated toward its midpoint triangle.

See also: Iterate (p. 178)

Working with Iterations

Once you've created an iteration and produced some iterated images, you can

- Select, color, hide, or delete the iterated images of individual objects within the overall iteration. For example, in the illustration above, you might wish to hide or delete the images of the iterated triangle's vertices, so that only the edges of the triangle are visible in your illustration.

- Alter the number of times the construction is iterated. Use **Properties** to visit the Iteration Properties dialog box of any iterated image, where you can adjust the number of iterations numerically.

- Adjust the number of iterations of a construction by first selecting one or more of its iterated images and then by pressing the + or − key to increase or decrease the number of iterations by one.

- Use the Iteration Properties dialog box to alter other properties of the iteration.

When defining new iterations, you can also use the Iterate dialog box to

- Create iterations in which each iteration step produces more than one copy of the pre-image. Such iterations allow you to create tessellations and fractals.

- Create iterations in which the depth of iteration is controlled by a parameter or other calculation in your sketch.

See also: Iterate (p. 178), Iteration Properties (p. 133), Multiple Iteration Maps (p. 182), Parametric Depth (p. 185)

Captions

Pythagorean Theorem

$a^2 + b^2 = c^2$

Chris Williams

Period 4

Use captions in Sketchpad to display text that identifies or explains your sketch. You can format captions to include a variety of sizes, styles, colors, and symbolic notation, and you can incorporate values from measurements, calculations, and labels of objects in captions.

Working with Captions

- Double-click the **Text** tool in empty space in your sketch to create and begin typing a caption.

- While you're editing, use the mouse or the arrow keys to move the insertion point or to select parts of the caption.

- Use the Text Palette to change the font, size, style, or color of the selected part of the caption.

- Click the Symbolic Notation tools in the Text Palette to add mathematical notation and formatting to your caption.

See also: Creating Captions (p. 88), Editing Captions (p. 88), Text Palette (p. 53)

Composite Captions

In some cases, you may want a caption to contain dynamic text—text that you do not type, but that Sketchpad provides automatically. A composite caption combines several different text elements into a single caption. The elements you can incorporate into composite captions include:

- other captions: The caption is incorporated as plain text.

- measurements and calculations: The current value of the measurement is incorporated, without the name or label.

- labeled objects: The label of the object is incorporated.

Using these elements, you could compose a single caption, such as "A 3 cm by 2 cm rectangle has an area of 6 cm²," from several other captions and measurements. As you alter your measured geometry, the composite caption dynamically updates to reflect the changed values in your sketch.

Creating a Composite Caption

To create a composite caption, select the objects you want to incorporate. At least one of the objects must be a caption, and each object must either be displayed as text or have a label. Then choose **Merge Text** from the Edit menu to create the caption.

Editing a Composite Caption

To edit a composite caption, separate the composite object into its parts using **Split Text,** make your changes to the parts, then recombine them using **Merge Text.**

See also: Creating Captions (p. 88), Editing Captions (p. 88), Text Palette (p. 53), Split/Merge (p. 115)

Action Buttons

Action buttons are objects you create in your sketch which you can press to perform a variety of actions, including hiding or showing objects, moving or animating objects, linking to a different page in your document or to a web site, scrolling the sketch window to a particular position, or making a presentation. Use action buttons to repeat frequent actions conveniently or to help explain the mathematics of your sketch to others who may interact with it.

Using Action Buttons

Create action buttons using the Action Button submenu in the Edit menu. Once you've created an action button, there are several things you can do with it.

Some buttons stay down after you press them, indicating that their action is still continuing. You can click such a button a second time to stop its action.

• Start the button's action by clicking the button body (not the handle) with the **Arrow** tool.

Handle   Body

• Select the button by clicking the handle (not the body) with the **Arrow** tool. Once the button is selected, you can hide it, delete it, and perform other actions on it.

• Change the button's font, size, style, and color by first selecting it, then using the Text Palette.

• Move the button to a different position by using the **Arrow** tool to drag the button's handle.

• Change the button's label by double-clicking it with the **Text** tool.

Hide/Show Buttons

A Hide/Show button hides or shows a group of objects.

Use Hide and Show buttons when there are details in a sketch which you sometimes want visible and sometimes want hidden. For example, your sketch might use a single triangle to show the construction of the circumcenter, centroid, and orthocenter. If you show all the construction lines at the same time, the sketch will be very confusing. You can use Hide/Show buttons to show or hide the construction lines for each of the three different constructions.

See also: Hide/Show Button (p. 112), Hide/Show Properties (p. 125)

Animation Buttons

An Animation button animates one or more objects. The objects must be either geometric objects or parameters.

Use Animation buttons to automate motion in your sketch. You can use an Animation button to move a point along its path, to move an independent point around randomly in the plane, or to vary a parameter. Use Animate Properties to set the animation speed and direction and to set the domain for parameter animation.

See also: Animation Buttons (p. 112), Animate Properties (p. 127)

Movement Buttons

`Move A -> B`

A Movement button moves one or more points toward defined destinations.

Use a Movement button to move an independent point or a point on path toward a specific destination.

See also: Movement Button (p. 113), Move Properties (p. 129)

Link Buttons

`Page 2`
`www.keypress.com`

A Link button links to a different page in the current document, or links to a web site or other location defined by a URL.

Use a Link button to make it easy to navigate among pages in a document that contains more than one page, or use a Link button to open up a web site that's related to the topic of your sketch.

See also: Link Button (p. 113), Link Properties (p. 130)

Scroll Buttons

`Scroll`

A Scroll button scrolls the sketch window so that a specific point in the sketch is located either in the center of the window or at the top left corner of the window.

Use a Scroll button in large sketches to position the window to show a particular part of your sketch.

See also: Scroll Button (p. 114), Scroll Properties (p. 133)

Presentation Buttons

`Present 2 Actions`

A Presentation button automatically activates a group of other buttons. The buttons can be activated either simultaneously or in sequence.

Use a Presentation button to choreograph a complex set of motions or to present a Sketchpad slide show.

See also: Presentation Button (p. 113), Presentation Properties (p. 130)

Pictures

Pictures are images not created by Sketchpad, which can be used to enhance or decorate a sketch.

To add a picture to your sketch:

1. Use some other program, such as Paint or a web browser, to create or locate an image you want to insert into your sketch.

2. Still using the other program, copy the image to the clipboard.

3. Switch back to Sketchpad.

4. Choose **Paste Picture** from the Edit menu. The picture appears in your sketch.

If, before pasting, you select one point, the top left corner of the picture will be attached to the point. If you select two points, the top left corner will be attached to the first point and the bottom right corner to the second point.

Hold down the Shift key while you drag to maintain the picture's original aspect ratio.

If you create the picture without selected points, the selected picture has resizing handles at the top left and bottom right corners. Drag these handles with the **Arrow** tool to resize the picture.

If you create the picture with a single selected point, there's only one resizing handle, at the bottom right corner.

If you create the picture with two selected points, there are no resizing handles. The positions of the two points determine how the picture is resized.

See also: Paste (p. 110), Resizing Pictures (p. 78)

Motion Controller

Use the Motion Controller to start objects animating and to control the motion of objects in your sketch.

Movement is at the heart of dynamic geometry. By animating and dragging objects in Sketchpad, you can rapidly explore many different variants of a construction, allowing you to make discoveries and investigate conjectures in a way that would be impossible without motion. Animation also allows you to demonstrate and present your findings in a more interesting and effective way than you could ever do with a static diagram.

Many of the functions of the Motion Controller are available through Sketchpad's menus, action buttons, and so forth. By providing a shortcut to these functions, the Motion Controller makes it quicker and easier for you to use animation in your sketch.

If you want even more control of animation than the Motion Controller provides, create Animation buttons as described in the Edit menu chapter (p. 112).

You use the Motion Controller to start objects moving, stop them, reverse their direction, and change their speed. It gives you easy access to the functionality of the **Animate, Increase Speed, Decrease Speed,** and **Stop Animation** commands in the Display menu, while providing better control of the speed and direction of moving objects. It makes it easy to control the motion of a specific moving object without affecting other moving objects.

The Motion Controller appears when you start an animation or when you choose **Show Motion Controller** from the Display menu.

When you move objects in Sketchpad, whether by using the Motion Controller, by choosing **Animate,** or by pressing an Animation or Movement action button, different objects move or change in different ways.

- Independent points move freely in the plane.

- Points on paths move along their paths.

- Parameters change their values.

- All other objects move by moving their parent objects.

See also: Animate (p. 150), Increase/Decrease Speed (p. 150), Stop Animation (p. 151), Show Motion Controller (p. 152), Animation Buttons (p. 36), Movement Buttons (p. 37), Object Relationships: Parents and Children (p. 10)

Motion Controller Elements

Each element of the Motion Controller affects a different aspect of motion.

You can also change the target by selecting an object with the **Selection Arrow** tool, although that can be hard to do if the object is moving.

Target: This button describes the objects that will be affected by the Motion Controller buttons. If at least one object is moving in your sketch, you can click to display a pop-up menu of moving points and changing parameters. Choose an object from the menu to select it and to make it the new target.

Target: Point A ▸ | Point A | Point B | Point C

If there are movable selected objects in your sketch, the target matches the selections. If there are selected objects that cannot be moved, there's no target. If the sketch contains moving objects but no selections, the target is all moving objects.

Animate: Click this button to animate each target object. This button has the same effect as the **Animate** command.

Stop: Click this button to stop each moving target object. This button has the same effect as the **Stop Animation** command.

Reverse: Click this button to reverse the direction of each moving target object. This button is enabled when at least one target object is moving in a fixed direction (rather than in random directions).

The Pause button affects all moving objects, not just the target.

Pause: Click this button to pause all motion. Unlike the other elements of the Motion Controller, this button affects every moving object, not just the target.

Speed: Click and type a new speed here to change the speed of each moving target object.

Speed: 1.0

Each speed step is a little more than 25%; three speed steps in a row changes the speed by a factor of two.

Increase/Decrease Speed Arrows: Click one or the other of these arrows to increase or decrease by one step the speed of each moving target. These arrows have the same effect as the **Increase Speed** and **Decrease Speed** commands.

Drag the Motion Controller by the title bar to reposition it. If you're using a Windows computer, you can also dock it to either the top or bottom of the Sketchpad window.

See also: Animate (p. 150), Stop Animation (p. 151), Increase/Decrease Speed (p. 150), Show Motion Controller (p. 152)

Using the Motion Controller

There are many different animation-related tasks you can accomplish using the Motion Controller.

Starting an Animation

The only objects you can't animate are captions, calculations, functions, action buttons, measurements, and pictures.

1. Select one or more objects you want to animate. The objects must be geometric objects or parameters.

2. Click the Animate button in the Motion Controller. Each selected object begins moving.

Selecting a Moving Object

If you want to modify the motion of a particular moving object, you must select that object to make it the target of the Motion Controller. If the object were not moving, you would simply click it with the **Arrow** tool to select it—but it's not always so easy to click a moving object.

You may be able to select the desired moving object with a mouse click if it's moving slowly or with a selection rectangle if there aren't any other objects near it. If not, follow these steps.

1. Press and hold on the Target menu to show the list of target objects.

2. If the object you want appears on the list, choose it. The object is selected, and you're done.

   If the object is not an independent point, a point on path, or a parameter, the object is moved by moving its parents, and it doesn't appear on the list. In this case, continue with steps 3 through 5.

3. Click the Pause button in the Motion Controller. Motion stops.

4. Select the object.

5. Click the Pause button again to release and restart the motion. The object remains selected and is listed as the target object.

Stopping a Moving Object

You can stop the motion of a single object while leaving other objects in motion.

Clicking Stop with nothing selected stops *all* moving objects.

1. Select the moving object as described in the previous section.

2. Click the Stop button in the Motion Controller. The selected object stops moving.

Reversing the Direction of a Moving Object

You can reverse the direction of any moving object as long as it's not animating randomly.

Clicking Reverse with nothing selected reverses *all* moving objects' directions.

1. Select the moving object as described in that section.
2. Click the Reverse button in the Motion Controller. The selected object reverses its direction.

Setting, Increasing, or Decreasing the Speed of a Moving Object

You can change the speed of any moving object.

When you have several objects moving at different speeds and you want to make all of them go faster or slower, use the speed arrows rather than typing a specific speed.

1. Select the moving object as described in that section.
2. To set the speed, click in the Motion Controller's speed control and type a new speed. The selected object moves at the new speed.
3. Alternatively, click on the up or down arrow in the Motion Controller's speed control. The selected object speeds up or slows down.

See also: Animate (p. 150), Stop Animation (p. 151), Increase/Decrease Speed (p. 150), The Arrow Tool (p. 70), Selection Rectangle (p. 71), Object Relationships: Parents and Children (p. 10)

Principles of Animation

The only objects you can't animate are captions, calculations, functions, action buttons, measurements, and pictures.

Just about every object you can create in Sketchpad can be animated. To animate an object, you can choose **Animate** from the Display menu, use the Motion Controller, or create an Animation action button. Of these three methods, action buttons give you the most control of the details of motion.

Different objects in Sketchpad move in different ways.

- Independent points move freely in the plane.

The default direction for points on most paths is bidirectional. For circle paths, however, the default direction is counter-clockwise—the direction of an opening angle.

- Points on paths move along their paths.

- Parameters change their values.

- All other objects move by moving their parent objects.

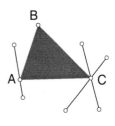

When you animate a geometric object that isn't a point, Sketchpad animates that object by animating its parents. For instance, if you animate a triangle interior, Sketchpad animates it by animating the vertices of the triangle. If one vertex is a point on path, it's moved along its path. If another is an independent point, it moves randomly on the plane. And if the third point is an object such as an intersection that isn't free to move, it's moved by moving its parents in turn. Thus, your ability to animate any conceivable geometric object is ultimately based on the animation of independent points and of points constructed on paths.

Most objects that display text (action buttons, measurements, calculations, functions, and captions) cannot be animated. The one exception is parameters. A parameter is like an independent point or a point on path in the sense that the value of a parameter, like the position of an independent point, does not depend on other objects. This means Sketchpad can animate the parameter by changing its value.

Because independent points, points on paths, and parameters are the only objects that can be animated independently of their parents, these are the only objects that Sketchpad directly animates, and they are the only objects that appear in the Motion Controller's Target pop-up menu. Other objects animate indirectly—by animating their parents.

Other objects can be listed as the Motion Controller target if they are selected. For example, if you select the interior of ΔABC, the triangle will be listed as the target. Even though the triangle is listed as the target, any motion changes you make will directly affect points A, B, and C and will affect the triangle indirectly.

See also: Points (p. 11), Point On Object (p. 153), Parameters (p. 19), Object Relationships: Parents and Children (p. 10), Animate (p. 150), Motion Controller (p. 39), Animation Buttons (p. 36), Animate Properties (p. 127)

Animation of an Independent Point

Merge independent points to paths if you want them to move in a specific direction.

An independent point is animated by moving it about in the plane. The animation speed determines how far it's likely to move in each random step. You cannot control the direction for an independent point. To specify the starting animation speed explicitly or to make the motion occur one time only, create an Animation action button that animates the point.

See also: Points (p. 11), Animate (p. 150), Motion Controller (p. 39), Animation Buttons (p. 36), Animate Properties (p. 127), Once-Only Motion (p. 46)

Animation of a Point on Path

To designate a specific portion of a line or ray as the domain for an animating point, construct a segment collinear with the line or ray and merge the point to the segment.

A point on path is animated by moving along its path. If the path is closed (for example, the interior of a circle, a polygon, or an arc) the animation proceeds around and around the path. If the path is a segment or an arc, the animation proceeds bidirectionally—back and forth along the path. If the path is infinite, as with a line or a ray, Sketchpad animates the point bidirectionally and tries to use the portion of the path that's visible in the window. To specify the direction or speed explicitly or to make the point travel its path only once, create an Animation action button that animates the point.

See also: Points (p. 11), Point On Object (p. 153), Animate (p. 150), Motion Controller (p. 39), Animation Buttons (p. 36), Animate Properties (p. 127), Once-Only Motion (p. 46)

Animation of a Parameter

A parameter is animated by changing its value within its domain. The default domain, direction, and speed of a parameter's variation depends on the units of the parameter, as shown in this table.

The speed listed here is a maximum. A parameter may change more slowly if your computer is busy with many tasks.

Units	Domain	Direction	Speed
None	−100 to 100 units	Bidirectional	1 unit/sec
Degrees	0° to 360°	Increasing	45°/sec
Radians	0 to 2π	Increasing	$\pi/4$ radians/sec
Inches	0 to 100 inches	Bidirectional	1 inch/sec
Cm	0 to 100 cm	Bidirectional	1 cm/sec

To specify the direction, domain, or speed explicitly, use the Parameter Properties panel or create an action button that animates the parameter.

See also: Parameters (p. 19), Parameter Properties (p. 125), Animate (p. 150), Motion Controller (p. 39), Animation Buttons (p. 36), Animate Properties (p. 127), Once-Only Motion (p. 46)

Motion Direction

The possible directions in which you can animate an object depends on the kind of object. When you start an animation using **Animate** or the Motion Controller, Sketchpad uses the most common direction for the objects you animate. To access more advanced direction choices, create an Animation action button.

A point on a path can be animated forward, backward, bidirectionally, or randomly. (If the path is a circle, the choices are counter-clockwise and clockwise instead of forward and backward.) If you specify random motion on a path, each time the point is moved it's given a brand-new random position somewhere on the path.

An independent point always moves randomly. Each time it moves, its new position depends both on its previous position and on its location relative to the window. A point moving slowly takes only small steps from its previous position, whereas a point moving quickly takes larger steps. If the point is near an edge of the window or outside the window, it's more likely to move toward the center of the window than away from it. In this way, independent points usually remain visible in the window while animating.

A parameter has a domain within which it is animated and can increase in value, decrease in value, change bidirectionally, or change randomly within that domain.

See also: Parameters (p. 19), Animation Buttons (p. 36), Animate Properties (p. 127)

Motion Speed

You can use the Motion Controller, the **Increase/Decrease Speed** commands, or an Animation button to set the speed of an animating object relative to the normal speed for that object.

You can set the ideal speed for points using **Advanced Preferences.**

The Motion Controller displays normal speed as speed 1.0. The actual velocity of normal speed depends both on your System Preferences and on your computer. Sketchpad attempts to keep this speed constant, but if your sketch is complex or your computer is busy with other tasks, normal speed may be slightly slower than requested in System Preferences.

See also: Motion Controller (p. 39), Increase/Decrease Speed (p. 150), Animation Buttons (p. 36), Animate Properties (p. 127), Parameters (p. 19), System Preferences (p. 140)

Once-Only Motion

When you create an Animation action button, you can specify that an object moves one time only. If the object is moving randomly, this means that one press of the button causes the object to move one time to a new random position. If the object is not moving randomly, once-only motion means that the object will stop once it returns to its starting position.

See also: Animation Buttons (p. 112), Animate Properties (p. 127)

Calculator

Use the Calculator to create or edit two kinds of Sketchpad objects: calculations and functions.

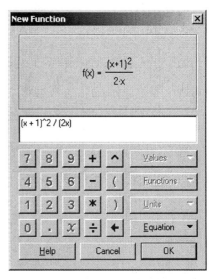

Calculations are values calculated using numbers, mathematical operations, functions, and measurements or other values from your sketch. These calculations can be used for a wide variety of purposes: to define distances, angles, and scale factors by which objects are transformed; to plot points; and to determine the results of other calculations and functions.

When you define a function in Sketchpad, you also use numbers, mathematical operations, functions, and measurements or other values from your sketch. Once you've defined a function, you can use it for various purposes: You can plot it, evaluate it, differentiate it, or use it to define other calculations or functions.

There are several different purposes for which you'll use the Calculator:

- To create a new calculation, choose **Calculate** from the Measure menu.

You can use the **Plot New Function** command to create a new function and plot it immediately.

- To create a new function, choose **New Function** from the Graph menu.

- To edit a calculation, double-click the calculation with the **Selection Arrow** tool; or select the calculation and choose **Edit Calculation** from the Edit menu.

- To edit a function definition, double-click the function with the **Selection Arrow** tool; or select the function and choose **Edit Function** from the Edit menu.

- To change a parameter into a calculation, select the parameter, choose **Edit Parameter** from the Edit menu, and change the expression to something more complicated than just a number.

- To change a calculation into a parameter, edit it so that it consists of one number only, with or without units.

See also: Calculate (p. 194), New Function (p. 202), Plot New Function (p. 203), Edit Definition (p. 119), Measurements, Calculations, and Parameters (p. 18), Functions (p. 27), Selection Arrow Tools (p. 70)

Parts of the Calculator

The Calculator has several parts: a keypad, an input line, a preview area, and a group of buttons for inserting special mathematical elements.

Keypad

Click the buttons in the Calculator's keypad to insert numbers, decimal points, operators, and parentheses into your calculation or function. Instead of clicking one of these buttons, you can also type the corresponding key on your computer's keyboard. (Use the / key—the forward slash—on the keyboard for division.)

The x key is present only when you're defining a function; it changes to y, θ, or r depending on the form of the equation.

Click the left-arrow key on the keypad, or the Backspace key (Windows) or Delete key (Macintosh) on the keyboard, to delete the last item you typed. If you're using the Calculator to define a function, you can click the key labeled x to enter the value of the independent variable.

Input Line

The input line displays each element you insert into the calculation or function as you enter it. Refer to the input line to see exactly what you've entered. You can also click in the input

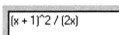

line or press the right- or left-arrow key on the keyboard to change the insertion point and add new numbers, operators, and so forth in the middle of an existing expression.

If the input line does not form a valid mathematical expression, the portion of the input line up to the first error is shown in black. The portion following the first error appears in red.

Preview Area

The preview area shows a mathematically formatted preview of the input line when it contains a valid expression. Use the preview to be sure that you've entered the desired calculation or function correctly—that you have

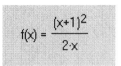

the parentheses in the right places and that you have the correct order of operations.

Pop-up Menus

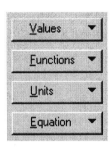

Depending on whether you're defining a calculation or a function, either three or four pop-up menus appear. The last of these, the Equation pop-up menu, appears only when you're defining or editing a function rather than a calculation.

You can click on an existing measurement or calculation in the sketch to insert it into the Calculator.

Values: This pop-up menu allows you to enter the value of any selected measurement in the sketch, to insert a new parameter, or to insert the value of the constant π or e. The values that appear in this menu include measurements or calculations that were selected in the sketch when the Calculator was opened. If you want to use a value from the sketch that doesn't appear in this menu, click on the value in the sketch to insert it into your expression. (If the value is hidden behind the Calculator, drag the Calculator by its title bar to move it out of the way and then click on the value.)

When you edit a calculation or function, you can insert only values that don't depend on the object you're editing. In other words, if you're editing a calculated value $2 \cdot AB$, and your sketch has another calculation which uses this result to calculate $2 \cdot AB + 2 \cdot CD$, you cannot insert the value of the second calculation into the first.

If you're defining a function, you can also use the Values pop-up menu to insert the value of the independent variable $x, y, r,$ or θ.

You can also click on an existing function that you've defined previously in the sketch to insert it into the Calculator.

Functions: This pop-up menu allows you to use in your expression any selected function you've already defined in the sketch, or to use any of Sketchpad's standard functions. Sketchpad's standard functions include the trigonometric functions, the inverse trig functions, and these additional functions:

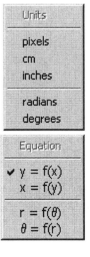

abs	Absolute value
sqrt	Square root
ln	Natural logarithm (base e)
log	Common logarithm (base 10)

The signum function is especially useful in creating a calculation that makes a decision based on the value of a variable, measurement, or parameter.

sgn	Signum (Returns +1, 0, or –1, depending on whether its argument is positive, zero, or negative.)
round	Round (Rounds its argument to the nearest whole number.)
trunc	Truncate (Truncates its argument by removing the fractional part. For example, trunc (2.6) = 2, and trunc (–7.8) = –7.)

Units: This pop-up menu allows you to insert any desired angle or distance unit (degrees, radians, inches, cm, or pixels). A unit must be attached to a number, so the Units menu is enabled whenever you've just inserted a numeric constant—either an ordinary number or one of the constants π and e.

See also: Plot Function (p. 203), New Parameter (p. 202)

Equation: This pop-up menu allows you to set the form in which the function appears. By setting the form of the function, you determine whether the independent variable is $x, y, \theta,$ or r. If you plot the function, the form you set here determines how the function plot appears. Choose $y = f(x)$ or $x = f(y)$ for a rectangular plot; or choose $r = f(\theta)$ or $\theta = f(r)$ for a polar plot.

See also: Plot Function (p. 203), Grid Form (p. 199)

How To . . . Use Signum to Construct a Piecewise Function

The signum function is useful any time you want a calculation which makes some sort of decision— which performs a different calculation when some value changes.

Sometimes you may want to construct a function that behaves one way in part of its domain and differently in another part of its domain. Such functions, called *piecewise* functions, are very important in interpolation, in fitting curves to data, and in designing and producing shapes and surfaces in applications such as automobile design. The signum function makes it possible to do this in Sketchpad.

For instance, you could construct a function whose plot is in the shape of a cosine wave when $x > 0$, but is parabolic when $x < 0$. Here's how to do this with the signum function:

1. Choose **Plot New Function** from the Graph menu.

2. Enter the cosine-wave part of the function, as shown at right. When $x > 0$, the signum function returns +1, and the value of the multiplier is 1. But when $x < 0$, the signum function returns –1, and the value of the multiplier is 0. This first part of the function will be a cosine wave to the right of the origin, but will always be zero to the left of the origin.

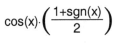

$$\cos(x) \cdot \left(\frac{1 + \text{sgn}(x)}{2} \right)$$

3. Enter the parabola part of the function as shown at right. When $x > 0$, the multiplier will be 0, and when $x < 0$, the multiplier will be 1.

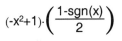

$$(-x^2 + 1) \cdot \left(\frac{1 - \text{sgn}(x)}{2} \right)$$

Here's the result when you click OK:

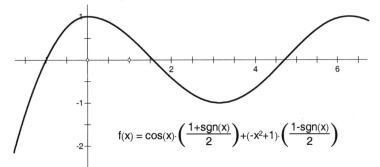

$$f(x) = \cos(x) \cdot \left(\frac{1 + \text{sgn}(x)}{2} \right) + (-x^2 + 1) \cdot \left(\frac{1 - \text{sgn}(x)}{2} \right)$$

The functions in this example were chosen in such a way that the two functions join continuously and smoothly. Can you construct a different piecewise function in which the join is not continuous, or in which it's continuous but not smooth?

Here's how to use the signum function to solve the general problem of defining a function $h(x)$ whose value is $f(x)$ for all $x < k$ and is $g(x)$ for all $x > k$:

$$h(x) = f(x) \left(\frac{1 - \text{sgn}(x-k)}{2} \right) + g(x) \left(\frac{1 + \text{sgn}(x-k)}{2} \right)$$

Inserting Values and Functions from the Sketch

If a value or function you want to insert is hidden behind the Calculator itself, drag the Calculator to the side so you can click on the object you want to insert.

While you're using the Calculator to define a calculation or a function, you can click existing values or functions in the sketch to insert these objects into your new expression. For instance, if you have a sketch in which you've already measured the length of segment AB, you can insert this length into the Calculator's expression by clicking on the existing measurement in the sketch. Similarly, if you have a sketch in which you've defined a function $f(x) = ax^2 + bx + c$, you can use this function in other calculations and functions by clicking on it in the sketch.

Inserting a New Parameter

While you're using the Calculator to define a calculation or a function, you can create a new parameter and insert it into your expression.

1. Choose **New Parameter** from the Values pop-up menu. A New Parameter dialog box appears.

2. Type the name you want to use for the new parameter. You can also set the initial value of the parameter.

3. Click OK. The parameter is inserted into your expression and added to your sketch.

See also: Parameters (p. 19), New Parameter (p. 202)

Text Palette

Use the Text Palette to format the font, size, style, and color of labels, captions, measurements, and other text. You can also use the Text Palette to insert mathematical symbols and formatting into captions.

The Text Palette can be used:

- when you have selected objects in your sketch and one or more of those objects either shows text or has a label. Use the Text Palette to change the appearance of the text or label of each selected object.

- when you're editing a caption and you have selected text in that caption. Use the Text Palette to change the appearance of the selected text.

Showing, Hiding, and Moving the Text Palette

Normally the Text Palette appears automatically when you edit a caption. You can turn this behavior on or off using the Text panel of **Preferences**. To show or hide the Text Palette manually, choose **Show Text Palette** or **Hide Text Palette** from the Display menu.

If you're using a Windows computer, the Text Palette normally appears attached (or *docked*) to the bottom of the Sketchpad application window. You can drag it to a different position and leave it either floating or docked to the top or bottom of the window. If you're using a Macintosh computer, the Text Palette always floats above or beside your document and can be repositioned by dragging its title bar.

On either kind of computer, when the Text Palette is floating, you can hide it by clicking its Close box, and you can move it to a different position on the screen by dragging its title bar.

See also: Show Text Palette (p. 53), Text Preferences (p. 137)

Using the Text Palette

The various parts of the Text Palette allow you to change the font, size, style, and color of labels and text. You can also use the Text Palette to add mathematical symbols and symbolic notation to your captions.

Text Palette

Pressing the down arrow triangles displays Font, Size, and Color pop-up menus.

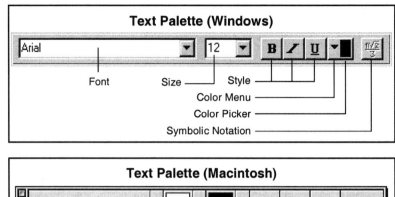

Text Palette (Windows)

Font · Size · Style · Color Menu · Color Picker · Symbolic Notation

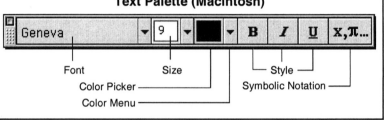

Text Palette (Macintosh)

Font · Color Picker · Color Menu · Size · Style · Symbolic Notation

Font: Change text font by choosing a font from the pop-up menu.

Size: Change text size by typing a size or by choosing a size from the pop-up menu.

Style: Change bold, italic, or underline text style by clicking on a button. One click sets the style and depresses the button; a second click removes the style and releases the button.

When a Text Palette color is applied to selected geometric objects, it affects the color of those objects' labels. To change the color of the objects themselves, use the **Color** command from the Display menu. (You can change the available colors by clicking Edit Color Menu in System Preferences.)

Color Menu: Change text color (to one of Sketchpad's default colors) by choosing a color from the pop-up menu.

Color Picker: Change text color (to any color your computer can display) by clicking this button to bring up your system's Color Picker dialog box.

Symbolic Notation: Display additional tools for mathematical notation by clicking here when you're editing a caption. Click a second time to hide the math formatting buttons.

See also: Captions (p. 34), Show Text Palette (p. 53), Advanced Preferences (p. 138), Color Picker (p. 63)

Using the Text Palette with Selections

To change the font, size, style, or text color of one or more labeled objects or objects displaying text, select those objects and use the Text Palette to make your desired modifications.

The Geometer's Sketchpad Reference Manual

Using the Text Palette While Editing a Caption

While you're editing a caption, select any portion of the text and set the font, size, style, and color using the Text Palette.

You can also enter mathematical symbols and mathematical formatting in a caption.

Entering Mathematical Symbols and Formatting

Press the Symbolic Notation button in the Text Palette to display additional notation tools you can use to enter mathematical symbols and other formatting, like overbars, fractions, exponents, and grouping symbols.

If you're using a Windows computer, you can drag these symbolic notation tools so that they're floating or so that they're docked to any side of the Sketchpad window. If you're using a Macintosh computer, these symbolic notation tools appear as a second row of buttons in the Text Palette.

The symbolic notation tools are divided into four groups.

Overbar Buttons: Click one of the overbar buttons to add a segment, a ray, a line, or an arc overbar to the selected text. These buttons are available only when there's text selected.

$$\overline{AB} \perp \overleftrightarrow{CD}$$

Operator Buttons: Click one of the operator buttons to add a fraction, square root, superscript (exponent), or subscript to the selected text. If there is no selected text, the operator is inserted with *?* symbols in the places which you need to fill in.

$$\sqrt{\dfrac{x^3}{5}}$$

Grouping Buttons: Click one of the grouping buttons to enclose the selected text in parentheses, square brackets, curly braces, or absolute value symbols. Unlike parentheses and brackets you type from the keyboard, mathematical grouping symbols always appear in pairs and resize automatically to fit whatever expression they enclose.

$$a\left(\dfrac{|x| + |y|}{2}\right)$$

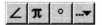
Symbol Buttons: Click one of the symbol buttons to insert an angle symbol, pi, the degree symbol, or any of

$$\alpha + \beta \geq \theta - \pi$$

the additional common symbols that appear in a pop-up menu when you press and hold on the last of these buttons.

You can combine the symbolic notation tools to add traditional mathematical notation to your captions or to invent new notations of your own.

To display symbolic notation, Sketchpad uses a special font containing mathematical symbols. By default, it uses the Symbol font that comes installed on every computer. If you wish to use some other font, you can change the Math Symbol font in System Preferences.

See also: Captions (p. 34), Text Palette (p. 53), Show Text Palette (p. 53)

Script View

The Script View offers an "inside look" at the workings of any custom tool. You should be familiar with using custom tools before working with the Script View.

The Script View window displays a readable description of the mathematical construction performed by a custom tool. Use the Script View to review the given object requirements of a particular custom tool, or to investigate how a tool was originally defined. In the Script View, you can add or read comments about the tool written by the tool's author; change properties—such as color or line weight—of the objects that the tool creates; and even apply the tool's construction in a step-by-step fashion to objects in your sketch.

To display the Script View window, choose **Show Script View** from the Custom Tools menu or click the Show Script View checkbox in the Document Options dialog box's view of custom tools. The Script View window sits on top of open document windows and displays the Script View of the most-recently chosen custom tool. To change the tool described by the Script View, choose a different custom tool from the available tools in the Custom Tools menu or in the Document Options dialog box.

Show Script View is only available when one or more custom tools have been added to your Custom Tools menu.

You can reposition the Script View by dragging its title bar and resize it by dragging its resize area. The Script View remains visible until you close it by choosing **Hide Script View** from the Custom Tools menu, or by clicking the window's close box.

See also: Custom Tools (p. 90), Tool Options (p. 104)

Tool Comment

The Tool Comment appears at the top of the Script View window, and contains any comments about the custom tool's purpose or behavior that its author chose to add. Adjust the size of the Tool

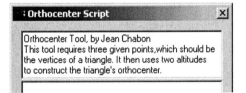

Comment by dragging the divider bar beneath it, and add to, or change the Tool Comment by typing. If you create new custom tools you plan to share with other Sketchpad users, use the Tool Comment to describe the tool's given objects, to identify yourself as the tool's author, and to explain how the tool should be used.

Any comments you add are saved with the tool, so you—or another Sketchpad user—can always refer to them when using the tool. When a Script View construction is printed, the comment is printed with the rest of the construction.

See also: Printing a Script View Construction (p. 62)

Object List

The Script View's Object List describes, in a step-by-step fashion, all of the objects and constructed relationships that make up the tool.

Given:

1. **Point A**

2. **Point B**

3. **Point C**

Steps:

1. Let $\overline{\textbf{AB}}$ = segment between A and B.

2. Let $\overline{\textbf{BC}}$ = segment between B and C.

3. Let $\overline{\textbf{CA}}$ = segment between C and A.

4. Let **j** = line perpendicular to $\overline{AB}$ passing through C (hidden).

5. Let **k** = line perpendicular to $\overline{CA}$ passing through B (hidden).

6. Let **D** = intersection of j and k.

The object list is divided into two major sections: Givens and Steps.

Given Objects

You can change the order of given objects by dragging individual given objects up or down in Script View.

The Given section shows all the given objects for the tool—all the objects that don't depend on any other objects in the tool. When using the tool in a sketch, these are the objects which you "match" in a sketch by clicking the tool. Given objects are listed in the order in which you must match them, which by default is the order chosen by the tool's author when the tool was created.

In some tools, the Given section may be divided into two parts, labeled Assuming and Given. The Assuming part contains assumed objects—given objects that are automatically matched to sketch objects having the same label when the tool is used in a sketch. The Given part contains the remaining given objects—the given objects that must be matched explicitly.

Assumed objects don't need to be matched explicitly when you use the tool, unless the sketch does not contain objects to match with the same label. (By default, a tool's given objects are explicit, as opposed to assumed. But when a tool is designed to be used repeatedly in the same sketch, in some situations the tool author finds it convenient to change some explicitly given objects into assumed objects to make the tool more convenient to use.) For more information about assumed objects and how to indicate them, see *Advanced Tool Topics* (p. 220).

Steps

The script step for an intermediate object describes it as "hidden."

The Steps section shows all of the objects, and the mathematical construction, defined by the tool's given objects. These include the tool's intermediate objects (which are not displayed when the tool is used in a sketch), and the tool's final results (which are displayed). Unlike given objects, a tool's steps cannot be reordered: they are determined by the tool's construction.

Working with the Object List

Use the Hidden checkbox in Object Properties to determine whether an object is an intermediate object or a result.

You can double-click any object in the Object List to change its properties. When you double-click, the Object Properties dialog box appears and you can use the various panels to make any desired changes to the properties. You can also use the Parents and Children pop-up menus on the Object panel to view and change the properties of the parents or children of the object.

You can right-click (Windows) or Ctrl-click (Macintosh) anywhere in the list to display a Context menu for the clicked object. Use this Context menu to change the color, line width, or tracing for the object on which you click. The Context menu also allows you to print the script.

See also: Object Properties (p. 121), Object Relationships: Parents and Children (p. 10), Automatically Matching a Given Object (p. 220), Printing a Script View Construction (p. 62)

Using a Custom Tool with the Script View

Use the Script View feedback to walk through a custom tool the first time you're trying a tool created by someone else.

If the Script View window is showing when you use a custom tool in a sketch, it provides visual feedback about the tool's use. Given objects that you've already matched with the tool appear highlighted. Given objects that you haven't matched yet appear after those you've matched, and are not highlighted. The object that the tool is currently matching appears between the two.

Applying the Script View Step-By-Step

Sometimes you may wish to apply a custom tool's construction to a sketch in a step-by-step fashion, rather than use it as a tool. If you are reasoning through the construction described in the Script View, for example, it's convenient to watch the construction occur in your sketch one object at a time. Likewise, if you're demonstrating a particular construction to your teacher or students, it may be useful to advance object by object. When you use a custom tool directly in the sketch, its constructed steps happen all at once, as soon as you've matched given objects, and only the tool's final results are displayed. But when you apply a Script View construction step-by-step, objects appear one at a time, and the construction's intermediate objects are temporarily displayed (so you can see them) until all steps are complete (when Sketchpad hides them for you).

To apply Script View's construction step-by-step to a particular sketch:

1. Use the **Selection Arrow** tool to select sketch objects that match the given objects displayed in Script View, in the order they appear in the Script View object list. For example, if the Script View lists three given points, select three matching points in your sketch.

   Assumed objects match automatically only when using custom tools directly, not when applying the Script View step-by-step.

   If the Script View displays both Assumed and Given objects, select matching objects first for the Assumed objects and then for the Givens.

As you select matching sketch objects, the Script View displays feedback about your selections. Given objects that match your selections appear highlighted; given objects for which you must still select matching sketch objects appear on a normal background.

2. Once you have selected objects to match all of the Script View given objects, two buttons appear at the bottom of the Script View window.

Click Next Step to apply the first step of the construction. Click this button repeatedly to walk through the entire construction, step-by-step. As each step is applied, the corresponding object appears in your sketch. While stepping through the construction, you can drag objects in your sketch to investigate their relationships to other objects.

Click All Steps to finish the construction by immediately constructing all remaining steps.

3. When the last step of the construction has been completed, the construction's intermediate objects—which the Script View temporarily displays in your sketch during stepping—are hidden, the results are selected, and the Next Step and All Steps buttons disappear. The Script View returns to its normal appearance.

If the tool's results match the givens, you can apply the tool repeatedly to its own results simply by clicking the All Steps button.

To apply the Script View construction a second time, select new matching objects as described in step 1.

During stepping, you can press the mouse on any already-matched given object or already-constructed step in the Script View to highlight the corresponding sketch object to which it matches. If you want to stop step-by-step application of the construction without completing All Steps, press the Esc key or close the Script View window.

See also: Object List (p. 58)

Printing a Script View Construction

When the Script View is showing, you can print its Tool Comment and Object List. Right-click (Windows) or Ctrl-click (Macintosh) on any object in the script, and choose Print Script View from the Context menu that appears.

Color Picker

The Color Picker dialog box allows you to choose a specific color to be used for displaying a Sketchpad object, for displaying text in Sketchpad, or for changing any of the colors available on Sketchpad's Color menu.

The Color Picker appears when you choose the **Display | Color | Other** command or when you click the Color Picker swatch on the Text Palette. It also appears when you click the Edit Color Menu button on the System panel of the Advanced Preferences dialog box.

The actual Color Picker dialog box is provided by the particular Macintosh or Windows operating system installed on your computer, and may differ from the sample dialog boxes shown below.

The Color Picker dialog box allows you to specify a color in several different ways. The most common methods involve RGB (Red-Green-Blue) values and HLS (Hue-Luminance-Saturation or Hue-Lightness-Saturation) values.

To specify a color using RGB, you set numeric values for the red, green, and blue components of the color. These numeric values are most commonly expressed either in percentages or in a range from 0 to 255, with higher numbers for a color corresponding to the presence of more of that color in the mix. Thus 255 for red and 0 each for green and blue specifies the purest possible red. Setting all three values to 0 specifies black (no color at all), and setting all three values to 255 specifies white (the brightest color, with the maximum amount possible of all three components).

The three values of HLS (Hue, Luminance, and Saturation) also allow you to specify a color numerically. Hue determines the color, such as red, blue, or green. Luminance determines how light or dark the colors are, with the maximum value corresponding to white and the minimum value (zero) corresponding to black. Saturation determines how much of the color is present; high saturation corresponds to vivid colors, and low saturation to pale colors. A saturation value of 0 specifies gray, with the shade of gray determined by the luminance. The most vivid pure colors correspond to the midpoint of the luminance scale and maximum saturation.

An alternative system called HSV (Hue-Saturation-Value) is similar to HLS, with the difference that the most vivid pure colors correspond to the maximum of the V scale (rather than the midpoint of the L scale) at maximum saturation. In this system white corresponds to zero saturation and maximum value.

See also: Other Color (p. 146), Text Palette (p. 53), Color Preferences (p. 136), System Preferences (p. 140)

Macintosh Color Picker

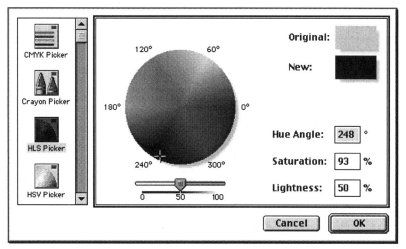

The Macintosh Color Picker lists on the left several different ways in which you can pick a color, including crayon colors, RGB, HLS and HSV.

If you use the HLS method, you can click anywhere in the color wheel to set the hue and saturation, with minimum saturation corresponding to the center of the wheel and maximum saturation to the edge of the wheel. Move the slider on the bottom to set the lightness.

Windows Color Picker

The Windows Color Picker shows at
the top the 16 colors available from
the Display menu's Color submenu.
The New Color swatch shows the
color that will be chosen if you click
the OK button.

Hue, Saturation, and Luminance allow
you to specify a color numerically.
The Hue value determines the color,
such as red, blue, or green. The
Saturation determines how much of
the color is present; high saturation
corresponds to vivid colors, and low
saturation to pale colors. Luminance
determines how light or dark the
colors are.

Alternatively, you can use the Red,
Green, and Blue values to specify a
color based on how much of each of
these primary colors is used.

Finally, you can use the rectangle and the vertical strip in the lower
portion of the dialog box to specify the hue, saturation, and luminance.
First click in the rectangle to choose the hue and saturation. Change the
hue by moving horizontally in the rectangle, and change the saturation
by moving vertically, with the minimum values at the bottom of the
rectangle and the maximum values at the top. Once you've chosen the
hue and saturation, click in the strip on the right to set the luminance.

Toolbox Reference

For thousands of years, since the time of Euclid, the fundamental tools of geometry have been the compass and the straightedge. Sketchpad's Toolbox includes these two tools—to construct circles and straight objects—and several other tools that allow you to select and drag objects, to construct points, to create and manipulate text and labels, and to define and manage custom tools. This section describes how to use each of the tools in Sketchpad's Toolbox.

Overview of the Toolbox

The Toolbox appears on the left of the screen when you start
Sketchpad, and includes six tools.

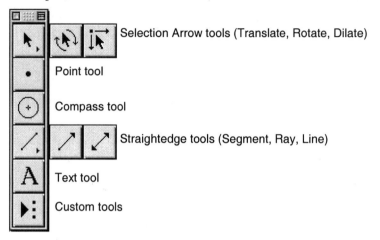

Selection Arrow tools (Translate, Rotate, Dilate)

Point tool

Compass tool

Straightedge tools (Segment, Ray, Line)

Text tool

Custom tools

- **Selection Arrow** tools: Use this tool to select and drag objects in your
  sketch. The three variations of the tool allow you to drag-translate
  (move), drag-rotate (turn), and drag-dilate (shrink or grow) objects.

- **Point** tool: Use this tool to construct points.

- **Compass** tool: Use this tool to construct circles.

- **Straightedge** tools: Use this tool to construct straight objects. The
  three variations of the tool allow you to construct segments, rays,
  and lines.

- **Text** tool: Use this tool to create and edit text and labels.

- **Custom** tools icon: Use this icon to define, use, and manage custom
  tools.

See also: Selection Arrow Tools (p. 70), Point Tool (p. 80), Compass Tool (p. 81),
Straightedge Tools (p. 83), Text Tool (p. 86), Custom Tools (p. 90)

Choosing and Using Tools

To use any of Sketchpad's tools, click the desired tool in the Toolbox.
Then move the mouse over the sketch and click or press and drag to
use the tool.

The **Selection Arrow** and **Straightedge** tools each come in three variations. To change from one variation to another, press and hold the **Selection Arrow** tool or **Straightedge** tool in the Toolbox until a menu pops out. Choose a different variation of the tool from this menu to make it active.

Windows users who have a mouse wheel can change the active tool by turning the wheel, and can switch between varieties of the **Selection Arrow** or **Straightedge** tool by pressing the wheel.

You can change the active tool by using the keyboard instead of the mouse. Hold down the Shift key and press the up or down arrow key to change the active tool. You can also hold down the Shift key and press the right or left arrow key to switch the **Selection Arrow** or **Straightedge** tool from one variation to another.

Once you've chosen a tool, that tool remains active until you choose a different one, so there's no need to click the same tool repeatedly to use it multiple times.

See also: Selection Arrow Tools (p. 70), Point Tool (p. 80), Compass Tool (p. 81), Straightedge Tools (p. 83), Text Tool (p. 86), Custom Tools (p. 90)

Using Tools to Scroll the Sketch Window

You can use any of Sketchpad's tools to scroll the sketch window and see different parts of the sketch. Hold down the Alt key (Windows) or the Option key (Macintosh) and press and drag in the sketch to scroll the entire sketch in the direction in which you drag. This feature works no matter which tool is active in the toolbox.

Hiding and Showing the Toolbox

You may want to hide the Toolbox when making presentations.

Hide or show the Toolbox by using the **Hide Toolbox** and **Show Toolbox** commands at the bottom of the Display menu.

See also: Hide/Show Toolbox (p. 152)

Moving, Resizing, and Docking the Toolbox

To move the Toolbox, (Windows or Macintosh) grab it by the title bar or (Windows only) by the gray area surrounding the buttons and drag it to a different location on the screen.

Windows users can dock the Toolbox to the left, top, right, or bottom edge of the application window. When the Toolbox is not docked, Windows users can also resize the Toolbox by dragging a border of the Toolbox window.

Selection Arrow Tools

The **Selection Arrow** tool is sometimes just called the **Arrow** tool.

The **Selection Arrow** tool is at the heart of Sketchpad's Dynamic Geometry capabilities—it's the tool you use to move (or *drag*) objects in your sketch. You'll drag objects to investigate mathematical relationships, to explore variations, to test conjectures, and to discover new properties.

You also use this tool to *select* objects in your sketch. Many of Sketchpad's menu commands act on selected objects. By selecting objects, you focus the software's attention on one or a handful of the many objects that make up a sketch. For example, you'll use selection to identify the objects to be transformed by the Transform menu or the objects to be measured by the Measure menu.

In addition to dragging and selecting, you can use the **Arrow** tool for several other purposes: constructing points of intersection, pressing action buttons, and resizing coordinate systems, function plots, pictures, and loci.

See also: Selecting and Deselecting Objects (p. 70), Dragging Objects (p. 73), Other Arrow Actions (p. 76)

Selecting and Deselecting Objects

You select objects in your sketch to drag them, to apply menu commands to them, or to manipulate or modify them with the Motion Controller or the Text Palette.

When a command is not available, it is grayed out in its menu. Often this means your current selection is not appropriate for that command.

At any point in time, your selections determine which menu commands are available at that point. For example, you can use the **Midpoint** command in the Construct menu when you have a segment selected, but not when you have a circle, a point, or a ray selected.

Your selections also determine how dragging works. If you select and drag both endpoints of a segment, the entire segment moves as a unit, with no change in its length or direction. But if you select and drag only one endpoint, the other endpoint remains fixed and the segment's length and slope change as you drag.

Selected objects appear outlined, or with special marks, as in the following illustrations.

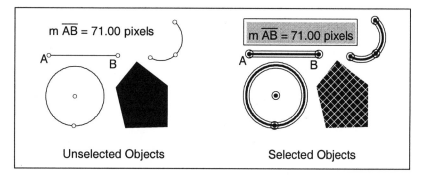

m $\overline{AB}$ = 71.00 pixels

Unselected Objects   Selected Objects

To select or deselect objects using a **Selection Arrow** tool:

The **Arrow** flips horizontal when it's pointing at an object.

- Select an unselected object by positioning the tip of the **Selection Arrow** over the object and clicking it.

- Select additional objects by clicking each object in turn.

- Deselect a single selected object the same way, by positioning the tip of the **Selection Arrow** over the object and clicking on it.

You can also deselect all objects by pressing the Esc key one or more times.

- Deselect all objects by clicking in empty space in the sketch.

In addition, you can:

- Select one of several overlapping or coincident objects by clicking repeatedly until the desired object is selected.

Clicking the body of an action button doesn't select it, but instead performs the action associated with the button.

- Select or deselect an action button by clicking its handle, not its body.

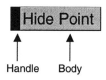

Handle   Body

- Select multiple objects simultaneously by enclosing them in a selection rectangle.

You can also select objects by using **Select All, Select Parents,** or **Select Children** from the Edit menu or by navigating to them using the Object Properties dialog box. You can select moving points by choosing them from the Motion Controller's Target menu.

See also: Midpoint (p. 154), Selection Rectangle (p. 71), Selecting Overlapping Objects (p. 72), Action Buttons (p. 35), Select All (p. 114), Select Parents (p. 115), Select Children (p. 115), Object Properties (p. 121), Motion Controller (p. 39), Esc Key (p. 209), Object Relationships: Parents and Children (p. 10)

Selecting Objects Using a Selection Rectangle

Use a selection rectangle to select multiple objects located near each other in a sketch.

1. Imagine a rectangle surrounding the objects you wish to select.

2. Position the tip of the **Selection Arrow** in empty space at one corner of this rectangle.

If you want previously selected objects to remain selected, hold down the Shift key while starting to drag the rectangle.

3. Press and hold the mouse button and drag diagonally toward the opposite corner.

   A dashed rectangle appears, and every object that the rectangle touches or encloses is selected.

4. When all desired objects are selected, release the mouse button. If you started your rectangle in the wrong place to select the desired objects, just begin again from step 2.

A properly positioned selection rectangle can be very useful for selecting multiple objects at once, for commands that apply to multiple objects, such as constructing the three midpoints of a triangle's sides, or for constructing a perpendicular.

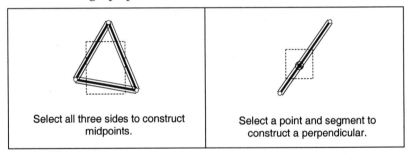

Select all three sides to construct midpoints.

Select a point and segment to construct a perpendicular.

See also: Selecting and Deselecting Objects (p. 70)

Selecting Overlapping Objects

Sometimes objects overlap or may even be geometrically coincident on the screen. If you want to select one of a set of coincident objects, here are some useful tips.

- Keep your eye on the status line at the bottom of the Sketchpad window. It will tell you which object you are about to select. If the object described isn't the one you want to select, try moving the **Arrow** around until the status line describes the desired object.

- If possible, point at a portion of your object that doesn't overlap other objects. In the following figure, for example, segment *CD* has been constructed collinear to line *AB*. You can select segment *CD* by clicking on the segment itself between points *C* and *D;* but to select line *AB*, it's easiest to click on the portion of the line *outside C* and *D*.

When you click overlapping objects, Sketchpad always selects points in preference to any other objects and always selects path objects in preference to interiors.

- If clicking selects the wrong object, click again in the same spot. A second click on similar overlapping objects will deselect the first object and select the next one. Keep clicking until you get the object you want.

- If clicking selects an object which isn't of interest to you and isn't important to the appearance of the sketch, choose **Hide** from the Display menu, then click again in the same spot.

- If all else fails, select a related object, use the **Properties** command to view Object Properties, and select the desired object using the Parents or Children pop-up menu.

To select more than one object of several located near each other on the screen:

- Use a selection rectangle to select all the overlapping objects.

- Select the first object, then hold down the Shift key while clicking additional objects.

See also: Selecting and Deselecting Objects (p. 70), Hide Objects (p. 146), Properties (p. 120), Object Properties (p. 121), Object Relationships: Parents and Children (p. 10)

Dragging Objects

Drag objects in your sketch for several purposes: to reposition the objects, to resize them, to change the shape of a construction, and to investigate the geometry embedded in the sketch, thereby discovering and revealing mathematical relationships between them. To drag an object, position the tip of the **Arrow** tool over the object, then press and drag.

The **Arrow** flips horizontal when it's pointing at an object.

- If the object was not selected, only that object drags. (Any other selected objects deselect.)

- If the object was already selected, it and all other selected objects drag to follow your mouse.

Sketchpad uses the terms *parent* and *child* to describe geometric relationships. A segment is the child of its endpoints; the endpoints are the parents of the segment.

When you drag an object, other related objects stretch and shrink to maintain their relationship to the dragged object. For instance, if you drag one endpoint of a segment, the segment stretches because the segment depends upon the location of both of its endpoints. Similarly, if you drag the segment itself, both endpoints move with it because the segment depends upon these endpoints and cannot move separately from them.

See also: Selecting and Deselecting Objects (p. 70), Object Relationships: Parents and Children (p. 10)

Transformations and Dragging

Mathematically, moving an object in your sketch *transforms* that object, and Sketchpad's dragging behavior is based on three geometric transformations: translation, rotation, and dilation. To allow you to use each of these transformations, Sketchpad actually has three **Arrow** tools: the **Translate Arrow** tool, the **Rotate Arrow** tool, and the **Dilate Arrow** tool. These three tools behave identically when used to select objects; it's only their dragging behavior that differs.

With the **Arrow** tool active, you can also switch transformations by holding down the Shift key and pressing the left or right arrow key on your keyboard.

When Sketchpad starts, the active **Selection Arrow** tool is the **Translate Arrow** tool. Choose a different **Arrow** tool, and a different transformation, by pressing and holding on the **Arrow** tool icon in the Toolbox. When you press and hold, a menu pops out and you can choose one of the three arrow tools.

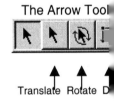

The Arrow Tool

Translate Rotate D

- Use the **Translate Arrow** tool to translate objects by any distance in any direction while maintaining their size, angle, and shape. (This is the default tool.)

- Use the **Rotate Arrow** tool to rotate objects about a center point, changing their angle while maintaining their size and distance from the center.

- Use the **Dilate Arrow** tool to dilate objects about a center point, only moving them closer to or farther from the center and making them correspondingly smaller or larger while maintaining their angle and shape.

See also: Dragging Objects (p. 73), The Translate Arrow Tool (p. 75), The Rotate Arrow Tool (p. 75), The Dilate Arrow Tool (p. 75)

The Translate Arrow Tool

Drag selected objects with this tool to translate them—that is, to slide them by any distance in any direction without turning or changing size or shape. This is the default **Arrow** tool.

You can use the **Translate Arrow** tool to select and deselect objects, press action buttons, and construct points of intersection just like the other **Selection Arrow** tools.

See also: Transformations and Dragging (p. 74), The Rotate Arrow Tool (p. 75), The Dilate Arrow Tool (p. 75), Translate (p. 170)

The Rotate Arrow Tool

Drag selected objects with this tool to rotate them—that is, to turn them around a center point by any desired angle without changing their distance from the center, their size or their shape.

You can also mark a point as the center of rotation by double-clicking it with an **Arrow** tool.

The center point used for rotation is the point you marked most recently using the **Mark Center** command. If you haven't marked a center point, Sketchpad automatically marks the point nearest to the center of the screen.

You can use the **Rotate Arrow** tool to select and deselect objects, press action buttons, and construct points of intersection just like the other **Selection Arrow** tools.

See also: Transformations and Dragging (p. 74), The Translate Arrow Tool (p. 75), The Dilate Arrow Tool (p. 75), Rotate (p. 174), Mark Center (p. 166)

The Dilate Arrow Tool

Drag selected objects with this tool to dilate them—that is, to stretch or shrink them farther from or closer to a center point by any desired amount without changing their direction from the center or their shape.

You can also mark a point as the center of dilation by double-clicking it with an **Arrow** tool.

The center point used for dilation is the point you marked most recently using the **Mark Center** command. If you haven't marked a center point, Sketchpad automatically marks the point nearest to the center of the screen.

You can use the **Dilate Arrow** tool to select and deselect objects, press action buttons, and construct points of intersection just like the other **Selection Arrow** tools.

See also: Transformations and Dragging (p. 74), The Translate Arrow Tool (p. 75), The Rotate Arrow Tool (p. 75), Dilate (p. 176), Mark Center (p. 166)

How To . . . Zoom In and Out on a Sketch

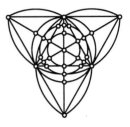

Sometimes a sketch may have so much detail that it becomes hard to select the object you want. Other times, a sketch may get spread out so that you can't see everything in the sketch window. If you want a **Zoom** command at such a time, you won't find it in Sketchpad's Display menu. However, you don't really need this command because Sketchpad has the **Dilate Arrow** tool, which is the mathematical equivalent of zooming.

To zoom in or out on a sketch, expanding it or shrinking it:

1. Choose **Select All** from the Edit menu to select everything in your sketch.

If you haven't marked a center point, Sketchpad marks one for you.

2. Use the **Dilate Arrow** tool to drag any selected object toward or away from the marked center. As you drag, your sketch zooms in or out.

See also: The Dilate Arrow Tool (p. 75), Select All (p. 114), Mark Center (p. 166)

Other Arrow Actions

Beyond dragging and selecting objects, the **Arrow** tool has several special actions when used with specific types of objects.

Arrow Tool Double-Click Shortcuts

Double-clicking the **Arrow** tool on several different kinds of objects quickly accomplishes the most common action for that kind of object. Double-clicking provides shortcuts for these actions that would otherwise require you to select the object and then choose a menu command.

Double-Clicked Object	Resulting Action
Point	**Mark Center** for rotations and dilations
Straight Object	**Mark Mirror** for reflections
Calculation	**Edit Calculation**
Function	**Edit Function**
Parameter	Allows you to change the parameter's value
Label	Shows Label Properties to edit the label
Caption	Begins editing the caption

See also: Mark Center (p. 166), Mark Mirror (p. 166), Label Properties (p. 122), Edit Calculation (p. 119), Edit Function (p. 119), Editing Captions (p. 88)

Arrow Tool Text Shortcuts

Often, you can use the **Arrow** tool with labels and captions without bothering to change to the **Text** tool. With the **Arrow** tool, you can:

• Press and drag a label.

• Double-click a label to edit the label with Label Properties.

• Double-click a caption to edit the caption.

See also: Text Tool (p. 86), Label Properties (p. 122), Editing Captions (p. 88)

Constructing a Point of Intersection

Click the **Arrow** tool on the intersection of two straight objects, circles, or arcs to construct a point at the intersection.

Clicking the **Arrow** tool at a potential point of intersection has the same effect as clicking the **Point** tool or using the **Intersection** command. So if you want to select an intersection that you haven't yet constructed, use the **Arrow** tool to construct and select it in one action.

See also: Point Tool (p. 80), Intersection (p. 155)

Pressing Action Buttons

Click the **Arrow** tool on the body of an action button to perform that button's action. (Different buttons have different actions: Some may cause an animation to start, others may hide or show objects, and so forth.)

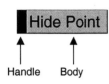

Handle   Body

When you point at the body of an action button, the cursor turns into a pointing finger indicating you are about to press the button. If you want to select or drag the button rather than perform its action, click on the handle of the button rather than its body.

If an action button performs an action that takes time to complete, it remains pressed until the action completes. Click the **Arrow** tool on the body of a pressed button to release it, halting the action in process.

See also: Action Buttons (p. 35)

Changing an Axis' Scale

Rescaling an axis lets you zoom in or zoom out on the coordinate system.

To rescale an axis or a coordinate system, click and drag any visible tick-mark number on the horizontal or vertical axis. When you position the **Arrow** tool over an axis' tick-mark number, the cursor turns into a bidirectional arrowhead, indicating you can drag to grow or shrink the scale of that axis.

If the coordinate system has square units, rescaling one axis will rescale the other. If the coordinate system has rectangular units, rescaling one axis has no effect on the other. If the coordinate system was defined in terms of fixed units, you will not be able to rescale it by dragging axis tick-mark numbers, as its scale is fixed by the quantities that define it.

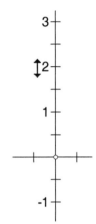

See also: Coordinate Systems and Axes (p. 21), Grid Form (p. 199), Define Coordinate System (p. 197)

Resizing Pictures

To resize a pasted picture:

1. Select the picture with the **Arrow** by clicking on it.

    A frame appears around the picture, indicating it's selected. In the upper left and bottom right corners of the frame, two small resize handles appear.

2. Click and drag one of the two resize handles.

    The picture begins resizing. Holding down the Shift key while dragging causes the picture to retain its original aspect ratio.

3. Adjust the picture to the desired size and stop dragging.

The Geometer's Sketchpad Reference Manual

If the picture was originally pasted onto a point to determine the location of its upper left corner, only the resize handle in the lower right of the selection frame will appear and be draggable. If the picture was originally pasted between two points, neither resize handle will appear, as the picture's location and size are determined by the positions of the points between which it is pasted.

See also: Pictures (p. 37), Paste (p. 110)

Resizing Function Plots and Loci

Function plots and certain loci display an arrowhead at one or both endpoints, indicating that the function plot or locus extends farther in the indicated direction than is presently displayed.

You can also set or change the domain of a function plot numerically in its Plot Properties panel.

You can resize such a function plot or locus—to extend farther or less far in the direction of an endpoint arrowhead—by dragging that endpoint arrowhead with the **Arrow** tool. As you point at the arrowhead, the cursor becomes a multidirectional arrow. Click and drag in the direction in which the arrowhead points to extend the locus or function plot; drag in the opposite direction to contract it.

See also: Functions and Function Plots (p. 27), Loci (p. 24), Plot Properties (p. 124)

Point Tool

Use the **Point** tool to draw or construct independent points, points on paths, and points at intersections.

- Click in an empty area of your sketch to create an independent point.

A point constructed on a path can move anywhere along the path, but nowhere else.

- Click on a path object—such as a segment, a circle, or the edge of a polygon interior—to construct a point on the path. When the **Point** tool is in the right place to construct a point on path, the path is highlighted, appearing thicker and in a special color.

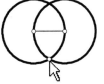

In addition to highlighting your targeted objects, Sketchpad displays a message in the status line (at the bottom of the window) telling you when you can construct a point on a path or at an intersection.

- Click at the intersection of two path objects—such as a segment and a circle, two lines or two circles—to construct a point of intersection. When the **Point** tool is in the right place to construct an intersection, both paths are highlighted, appearing thicker and in a special color.

There are several ways to create points without using the **Point** tool. For example, clicking with the **Arrow** tool on an intersection constructs a point of intersection there in the same way the **Point** tool does. The **Compass** tool, **Straightedge** tools, and most **Custom** tools sometimes construct their own points as part of their operation. The **Point On Object**, **Midpoint**, and other menu commands also construct points.

See also: The Toolbox (p. 69), Points (p. 11), Path Objects (p. 13), Selection Arrow Tools (p. 70), Compass Tool (p. 81), Straightedge Tools (p. 83), Custom Tools (p. 90), Point On Object (p. 153), Midpoint (p. 154), Intersection (p. 155)

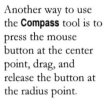

Compass Tool

Use the **Compass** tool to construct circles determined by two points—the center point and another point through which the circle passes. This second point is sometimes called the *radius point*, because it determines the radius of the circle.

Constructing a Circle

1. Choose the **Compass** tool if it's not already active.

Another way to use the **Compass** tool is to press the mouse button at the center point, drag, and release the button at the radius point.

2. Click to locate the center of your circle. (You can click in empty space, on an existing point, on a path object such as a segment or another circle, or on an intersection.)

3. Click again to locate the radius point.

Attaching a Circle to an Existing Object

You can attach either the center point or the radius point to an existing object. To do so, you can click on

- an existing point

- a path object (such as a segment, a line, a circle or an arc)

- an intersection of two path objects.

When the **Compass** tool is in the right place to click on an existing object, that object is highlighted, appearing thicker and in a special color.

Be careful when you want to attach the radius point of a circle to an existing object. It's not enough to position the circle so that the circle appears to go through the desired point. You must actually position the tool itself over the point or object to which you want to attach before clicking or releasing to locate the radius point.

In the left box of the following illustration, even though the circle appears to pass through the vertices of the triangle, the radius point will be located in empty space. The result is that the radius point will be independent, and dragging either the radius point or any part of the triangle will show that the circle isn't attached to the vertices.

In the right box of the same illustration, the tool is positioned at a vertex, and the vertex is highlighted. Thus, that vertex will be the radius point of the circle, and the size of the circle will be linked to the position of the vertex no matter how various parts of the figure are dragged.

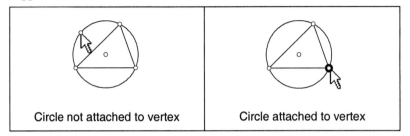

| Circle not attached to vertex | Circle attached to vertex |

Related Commands

There are two Construct menu commands that construct circles without using the **Compass** tool.

- **Circle By Center+Point** constructs a circle determined by two selected points. The first point is the center point, and the second is the radius point.

The selected distance can be either a segment or a distance measurement.

- **Circle By Center+Radius** constructs a circle determined by a selected point and a selected distance. The selected point is the center point, and the selected distance determines the radius.

See also: The Toolbox (p. 69), Circles (p. 15), Path Objects (p. 13), Circle By Center+Point (p. 158), Circle By Center+Radius (p. 159)

Straightedge Tools

Use the **Straightedge** tools to construct straight objects: segments, rays, and lines. Each straight object constructed by one of these tools is determined by two points.

A straightedge is a ruler without marks. It can be used for drawing straight lines but not for measuring.

Use the **Segment** tool to construct a segment between its two endpoints.

Use the **Ray** tool to construct a ray from one endpoint through another point.

Use the **Line** tool to construct a line through two points.

With any **Straightedge** tool active, you can switch to other **Straightedge** tools by holding down the Shift key and pressing the left or right arrow key on your keyboard.

When Sketchpad starts, the active **Straightedge** tool is the **Segment** tool. Choose a different **Straightedge** tool by pressing and holding on the **Straightedge** tool icon in the Toolbox. When you press and hold, a menu pops out and you can choose any of the three tools.

To Construct a Segment:

1. Choose the **Segment** tool if it's not already active.

2. Click to locate the first endpoint of the segment. (You can click in empty space, on an existing point, on a path object such as another segment or a circle, or on an intersection.)

3. Click again to locate the second endpoint.

If you prefer, you can use any of the **Straightedge** tools by pressing the mouse button at the location of the first point, dragging the mouse, then releasing the mouse button at the location of the second point.

To Construct a Ray:

1. Choose the **Ray** tool if it's not already active.

2. Click to locate the endpoint of the ray. (You can click in empty space, on an existing point, on a path object such as a segment or another circle, or on an intersection.)

3. Click again to locate the point through which it travels.

To Construct a Line:

1. Choose the **Line** tool if it's not already active.

2. Click to locate a first point through which the line travels. (You can click in empty space, on an existing point, on a path object such as a segment or another circle, or on an intersection.)

3. Click again to locate a second point through which the line travels.

Attaching a Straight Object to an Existing Object

You can attach either the first or second determining point of a straight object to an existing object. To do so, you can click

- an existing point

- a path object such as a segment, a line, a circle, or an arc

- an intersection of two path objects.

When the **Straightedge** tool is in the right place to click on an existing object, that object is highlighted, appearing thicker and in a special color.

Be careful when you want to attach a defining point to an existing object. It's not enough to position the tool so that the ray or line appears to go through the desired location. You must actually position the tool itself over the object to which you want to attach before clicking or releasing the mouse to locate the defining point.

For example, a student wants to draw a diagonal line passing through the intersection of the horizontal and vertical lines. In the following illustration, even though the line in the left box appears to pass through the intersection, the cursor is positioned to click in empty space, so the second defining point of the line won't be attached. But the cursor in the right box is over the intersection, so the intersecting lines are highlighted, and when clicked on, the point will be defined at the intersection.

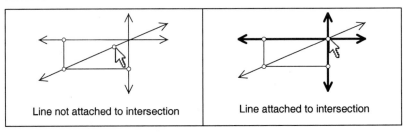

| Line not attached to intersection | Line attached to intersection |

In another example, a student wants to attach a ray's *through* point to the circle so the through point can be animated around the circle. The next illustration shows how to accomplish this. Positioning the cursor to click where shown in the left box won't work because the through point will not be attached to the circle. Clicking where shown in the right box, with the cursor over the circle and the circle highlighted, defines the point on the circle.

The Geometer's Sketchpad Reference Manual

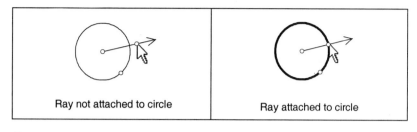

| Ray not attached to circle | Ray attached to circle |

Constructing Straight Objects at Specific Angles

While you're constructing a straight object, you can hold down the Shift key to make the object horizontal, vertical, or at an angle of 15°, 30°, 45°, 60°, or 75°. Construct the second point before you release the Shift key.

Related Commands

There are several commands in the Construct menu that construct straight objects without using the **Straightedge** tool.

- **Segment, Ray,** and **Line** commands construct straight objects determined by two or more selected points.

- **Perpendicular Line** and **Parallel Line** construct a line through a selected point that is perpendicular or parallel to a selected straight object.

- **Angle Bisector** constructs a ray that bisects the angle formed by three selected points.

See also: The Toolbox (p. 69), Straight Objects (p. 155), Path Objects (p. 13), Segment (p. 83), Ray (p. 83), Line (p. 83), Perpendicular Line (p. 157), Parallel Line (p. 156), Angle Bisector (p. 158)

Text Tool

Use the **Text** tool to perform a variety of operations on labels and on other objects that display text.

Text plays an important role in Sketchpad. Measurements and calculations allow you to determine and communicate important information about the geometric objects in your sketch. Labels provide the correspondence between measurements and the objects they measure and allow you to communicate with others about specific objects in your sketch. Captions allow you to identify and describe both your sketch as a whole and individual parts of your sketch. Sketchpad's functions are fundamental mathematical objects expressed symbolically—another form of (mathematical) text. And parameters provide a convenient way to change the behavior of both geometric objects and functions.

See also: Captions (p. 34), Measurements (p. 18), Functions (p. 27), Parameters (p. 19)

Using the Text Tool

Use the **Text** tool to create, show, hide, and edit labels, to create and edit captions, and to change the text displayed with measurements, calculations, and parameters.

The **Text** tool has four possible appearances when you move the mouse over the sketch. These appearances depend on what it's pointing at and indicate the effect of using the tool.

Objects like points and circles can either show or not show a label. Some other objects—like action buttons or parameters—always show their label. And some other objects—like captions and pictures—never show a label.

Filled hand: Click to show or hide the label of the object at which you're pointing. This cursor appears only when you're pointing at an object that has a label to show or hide.

Labeled hand: Press and drag to reposition the label of a geometric object or double-click to edit the label of the object you're pointing at. This cursor appears when you're pointing at a label or at a text object (such as a parameter or a measurement) that can be labeled.

Open hand: Double-click to create a new caption. This cursor appears only when you're pointing at empty space or at an object that never displays text.

I-beam: Click, press and drag, or double-click to edit a caption. This cursor appears when you're pointing at a caption.

See also: Show/Hide Label (p. 147), Positioning and Changing Labels (p. 88), Creating Captions (p. 88), Editing Captions (p. 88), Text Preferences (p. 137)

Showing and Hiding Labels

When you point the **Text** tool at a geometric object, the tool appears as a filled hand.

By default, objects are labeled automatically when you measure them. (Use Text Preferences to turn off this feature.) You can also change Text Preferences so that all new points are labeled when they're created.

- Click to show the object's label.

- Click again to hide the object's label.

Here are the default labels Sketchpad uses for various kinds of objects (before you change them):

Object	Default Label
Point	A, B, C, …
Straight Object	j, k, l, …
Circle	c_1, c_2, c_3, …
Circle Interior	C_1, C_2, C_3, …
Arc	a_1, a_2, a_3, …
Arc Interiors	A_1, A_2, A_3, …
Polygon*	P_1, P_2, P_3, …
Point Locus	L_1, L_2, L_3, …
Non-point Locus	Cannot show a label
Function	f, g, h, …
Function Plot	$y=f(x)$, …
Measurement	m_1, m_2, m_3, …
Parameter	t_1, t_2, t_3, …
Caption	Cannot show a label
Pictures	Cannot show a label
Action Buttons	Label depends on action

*When possible, a polygon with six or fewer vertices is labeled according to its vertices.

If Sketchpad runs out of letters with which to label points or straight objects, it starts over with A_1 and j_1.

See also: Show/Hide Label (p. 147)

Positioning and Changing Labels

 When you point the **Text** tool at an object's label or at a measurement, parameter, calculation, or function, the tool appears as a labeled hand.

Double-clicking is the same as choosing **Properties** from the Edit menu, then showing the Label panel.

- Double-click to change the label.

- Press and drag to reposition the label of a geometric object.

You can also change the font, size, style, and color of selected objects' labels with the Text Palette or with text commands in the Display menu.

See also: Properties (p. 120), Label Properties (p. 122)

Creating Captions

When you point the **Text** tool at an empty place in the sketch, the tool appears as an open hand.

- Double-click to create and begin typing and editing a new caption.

To finish editing your caption, press the Esc key or click anywhere outside the caption.

See also: Captions (p. 34), Editing Captions (p. 88), Show/Hide Text Palette (p. 151), Text Palette (p. 53)

Editing Captions

I When you point the **Text** tool at a caption, the tool appears as an I-beam.

- Click to place an insertion point and begin editing.

- Press and drag to select a block of text to replace.

- Double-click to select the word under the cursor.

You can turn off this default behavior using Text Preferences, and instead use **Show Text Palette** to summon the Text palette as needed.

When you create a caption, by default Sketchpad displays the Text Palette. You can change the font, size, style, or color of selected caption text by using this palette or by using text commands in the Display menu. The Text Palette also contains symbolic notation tools for adding mathematical text to your caption.

To finish editing, press the Esc key or click anywhere outside the caption.

See also: Captions (p. 34), Text Palette (p. 53), Display Menu (p. 143), Show/Hide Text Palette (p. 151)

Custom Tools

The **Custom** tool icon allows you to define and use custom tools.

Overview of Custom Tools

Custom tools are tools that you create yourself or that other Sketchpad users create for you. In just the way that Sketchpad's **Compass** tool constructs a circle given its center and radius point, custom tools that you create can construct figures of arbitrary complexity. For example, you can make a custom tool that constructs the perpendicular bisector of a given segment, or one that constructs the circumcircle of a given triangle, or one that constructs a square given two adjacent vertices. A more advanced custom tool might create a fractal, or a tangent to an arbitrary point on a function plot, or a complex tessellation. Any custom tool you define can be used an unlimited number of times in an unlimited number of sketches. By defining new custom tools, you extend the built-in tools available to you in Sketchpad. Since you can create any type or number of custom tools you wish, the possibilities for extending Sketchpad's tools are limitless.

Tools that you create reside inside the document in which you create them. You can always use them in that document (unless you remove them from that document) just as if you were using a built-in tool like the **Compass** or **Straightedge**. When a document containing custom tools is open, you can also use those tools in any other open document. Finally, you can place documents containing frequently used tools inside a special Tool Folder on your hard drive. Any tools in your Tool Folder will be available all the time, even when the documents that contain them are not open in Sketchpad.

Custom Tools Menu

When you press the **Custom** tool icon in the Toolbox, Sketchpad displays the Custom Tools menu. This menu has several parts.

Create New Tool. This command defines a new custom tool based on your selections in the sketch.

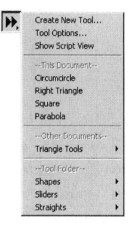

Tool Options. This command allows you to organize, rename, copy, or remove the custom tools contained in your sketch.

Show Script View. This command shows or hides the most recently chosen custom tool's script—a step-by-step description of what the tool constructs. The command is **Hide Script View** if the script is already showing.

This Document. This part of the menu lists all of the custom tools defined in the current (active) document. If the active document does not yet contain any tools, this part of the menu does not appear. When you define a new custom tool, it appears first in this part of the menu.

Other Documents. This part of the menu lists all of the other open documents that contain custom tools. Each entry in this part of the menu lists an open document that contains tools and displays a submenu of each of the tools in that document. If no other open documents contain tools, this part of the menu does not appear.

Tool Folder. This part of the menu lists any tools from documents that were stored in the Tool Folder when Sketchpad started. This folder is a special folder (directory) named **Tool Folder** that's stored next to the Sketchpad application on your hard disk. If no documents were stored in this folder when Sketchpad started (or if the documents in this folder didn't contain any tools), this part of the menu does not appear.

When you want to define a new tool or reorganize your tools, use the commands at the top of this menu. When you want to use a tool to construct objects in your sketch, choose it from one of the lower parts of the menu. The chosen custom tool then becomes active until you choose a different tool, just as if you'd chosen the **Compass** or

Straightedge tool. (In other words, if you want to use the same custom tool several times in a row, you don't need to choose it again from the Custom Tools menu.) If you've switched from a custom tool to some other tool, such as the **Arrow**, you can switch back to the last custom tool you used by clicking—rather than pressing—on the **Custom** tool icon. This activates the most recently chosen, checkmarked tool. If you want to switch from one custom tool to another or from a built-in tool, such as the **Arrow**, to a new custom tool, choose the new tool from the Custom Tools menu.

See also: Using a Custom Tool (p. 92), Making a Custom Tool (p. 94), Advanced Tool Topics (p. 220), Document Tools (p. 7), Show Script View (p. 106), Script View (p. 57)

Using a Custom Tool

Custom tools are easy to use, even before you learn to make one yourself. In this example, you'll use custom tools that are already defined in one of the sample documents that comes installed with Sketchpad. The document **Sample Tools.gsp** contains several custom tools. Just by opening that document, you can use its tools in your own sketch.

1. Open the document **Sketchpad | Samples | Custom Tools | Sample Tools.gsp**.

2. Press and hold on the **Custom** tools icon in the Toolbox. The Custom Tools menu appears.

3. Choose **Circumcircle** from the menu. This custom tool constructs a triangle and its circumcircle given three points.

4. Move your mouse over the sketch and click in three different places. A triangle appears with its circumcircle—the circle that passes through all three vertices.

5. Continue using the **Circumcircle** tool. Click three more times in the sketch for each triangle you want to construct. You can click in empty space, on existing points, on paths, or on intersections just as you can with the **Point, Compass,** and **Straightedge** tools.

You can also press, drag, and release to get the same effect as two clicks (one where you pressed, and one where you released).

6. When you're finished making triangles with circumcircles, click on any other tool in the Toolbox or press the Esc key.

To resume making circumcircles, click the **Custom** tool icon again. You don't need to press and hold to choose from the Custom Tools menu the next time—just click the **Custom** tool icon to activate it. Press and hold the **Custom** tool icon in the Toolbox only when you want to switch to a different custom tool from the menu.

See also: The Givens and Results of a Tool (p. 93), Matching Given Objects (p. 93), The Tool Folder (p. 98), Custom Tools Menu (p. 91)

The Givens and Results of a Tool

The **Circumcircle** tool has three givens—the vertices of the triangle. The three sides of the triangle and the circumcircle are the tool's results.

Each time you click as you use a tool, you are specifying a *given object*—an object that is used to determine the rest of the objects the tool produces. The objects produced by the tool (that depend on the given objects) are the *results* of the tool.

You can think of the various objects and relationships that make up a tool as a family tree. In this family tree, the givens are the ultimate ancestors—objects that have children but no parents. The other objects—those that have parents—are the results of the tool.

See also: Object Relationships: Parents and Children (p. 10)

Matching Given Objects

The status line can help you figure out what to match next.

Tools can use as their givens various kinds of objects: points, straight objects, circles, measurements, functions, and so forth. When you use a tool, a message appears on Sketchpad's status line at the bottom of the window describing what kind of given object you need to match next.

For example, if a tool uses a point, a segment, and a distance measurement as its three givens, the status line first says "1. Match Point…" to indicate what object you must match first. After you match the point, the status line says "2. Match Segment…" to indicate that you must next specify a segment. And finally, it says "3. Match Distance Measurement…" when it's time for you to click on a distance measurement as the last given object.

You can always match a given by clicking on a sketch object of the correct kind. For some givens—points, straight objects, and circles—you can also match the given by constructing it.

If a given object for a tool is a point, you can specify it in either of two ways.

- Specify an existing point: Click on an existing point in the sketch. The point you click on is used as the given.

- Construct a new point: Click somewhere else in the sketch—in empty space, on a path, or at an intersection—to construct a new point. The point you construct is used as the given.

If a given object for a tool is a circle or straight object, you can specify it in either of two ways.

- Specify an existing object: Click on an existing object of the correct kind. The object you click on is used as the given.

- Construct a new object: Click twice (or press and drag) in the sketch to specify the two points which determine the given. If you're constructing a circle given, the first point is the center and the second point is the radius point. If you're constructing a straight object, the two points are the two determining points of the straight object.

If the given for a tool is any other kind of object, you must click on a matching object in the sketch. If no object of the correct kind exists in the sketch, you must create such an object before you can use the tool.

Making a Custom Tool

You define new custom tools *by example:* you create a construction you wish to "turn into a tool," then define a tool based on that example. Turn any construction into a custom tool by selecting sketch objects that define a construction you wish to turn into a tool. The objects you select must be related to each other in such a way that at least one selected object is completely determined by other selected objects. Then choose **Create New Tool** from the Custom Tools menu.

The selected objects to be produced by a tool are called *results.* The selected objects that don't depend on any others, but upon which the results depend, are called *givens.* Any unselected objects that relate the selected givens to the selected results are *intermediate objects.* (Intermediate objects are not reproduced when you use the tool; only the objects that were selected when you defined the tool are reproduced as results when you use the tool.)

Follow these steps to make a new custom tool:

1. Make a construction to serve as an example of the construction you want the tool to produce. You can use any of Sketchpad's tools or menus to create this exemplar.

2. Select both the given objects (usually, independent points) and the desired resulting objects you'd like the tool to produce. The order in which you select the givens determines the order in which you'll match givens when using the tool.

3. If there are other objects that relate the givens to the final results, you can select them or not. If you do select them, they will be shown when you use the tool. If you don't select them, they won't appear when you use the tool.

4. Choose **Create New Tool** from the Custom Tools menu that appears.

5. A dialog box appears in which you can type a name for the tool. Type a name and click OK.

Your tool is added to the Custom Tools menu, and is ready to use.

See also: Custom Tools Menu (p. 91)

Specifying the Results of a Tool

When you make a tool, any selected objects that depend on the givens become results of the tool, and will be shown when you use the tool. Any unselected objects that depend on the givens will not be shown when you use it.

For example, if you make a tool that constructs the perpendicular bisector of a segment, the segment is the given object and the perpendicular bisector is a result. If you select the midpoint of the segment when you make the tool, the midpoint is also a result, and is shown when you use the tool. If you don't select the midpoint, it's an intermediate object and is hidden when you use the tool.

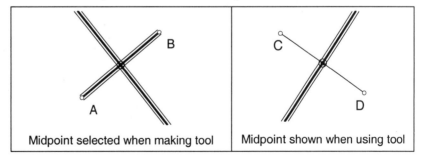

| Midpoint selected when making tool | Midpoint shown when using tool |

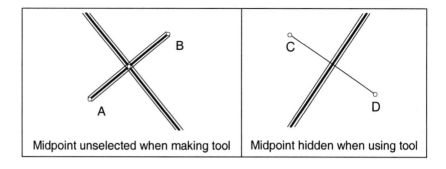

| Midpoint unselected when making tool | Midpoint hidden when using tool |

See also: Custom Tools Menu (p. 91)

Managing Custom Tools

After you've created one or more custom tools in a document, you can rearrange them, copy them to other documents, rename them, or remove them by choosing **Tool Options** from the Custom Tools menu. This command opens the Document Options dialog box to a view of your document's tools. See **Document Options** for more information.

See also: The Givens and Results of a Tool (p. 93), Using a Custom Tool (p. 92), Advanced Tool Topics (p. 220), Document Options (p. 104), Custom Tools Menu (p. 91)

Showing or Hiding the Script View

Choose **Show Script View** or **Hide Script View** from the Custom Tools menu to show or hide the script view of the active tool. This view allows you to see the given objects and the steps the tool takes to construct its results, as well as, to change the properties of the steps, and to observe and control the tool as it functions.

See also: Script View (p. 57), Custom Tools Menu (p. 91)

How To . . . Make a Perpendicular Bisector Tool

If you're doing an investigation in which you need to construct several perpendicular bisectors, you can make a perpendicular bisector tool to simplify your work. Suppose you want to construct the perpendicular bisectors to all three sides of a triangle. Rather than do the perpendicular bisector construction three times, you can do it once and make it into a tool. Then you can use the tool for the other two perpendicular bisectors. This example shows you how.

1. In a new document, use the **Segment** tool to construct $\triangle ABC$.

2. On segment AB, construct the midpoint and the perpendicular to segment AB through the midpoint.

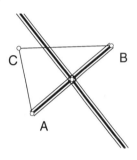

Segment AB is the given object, and the midpoint and perpendicular are results.

If you had also selected points A and B, they would have been the givens, and the segment would have been an intermediate result.

3. Select segment AB, the midpoint, and the perpendicular line.

4. Press and hold the **Custom** tool icon and choose **Create New Tool** from the Custom Tools menu that appears.

5. Type `Perpendicular Bisector` to name your tool and click OK.

6. Click the **Custom** tool icon to choose your new tool.

7. Click on each of the other two sides of the triangle. The tool constructs the perpendicular bisectors on those two sides.

8. Press the Esc key or choose a different tool from the Toolbox to stop using your custom tool.

Because the given of this tool is a segment, you can match it either by clicking on a segment, as you did above, or by clicking twice (or pressing and dragging) to construct a new segment to match the given. This means you can use the tool to construct a triangle from scratch with the perpendicular bisectors constructed automatically.

1. Click the **Custom** tool icon to choose your **Perpendicular Bisector** tool.

2. Press in empty space in the sketch and drag to construct one side of a triangle.

3. Press and drag two more times to construct the remaining two sides of the triangle.

You've just constructed a triangle, as easily as you'd have done it with the segment tool, but with perpendicular bisectors on all three sides.

Use your new tool to construct a quadrilateral with the perpendicular bisectors of all four sides. Then construct one diagonal, along with its perpendicular bisector. What do you notice about the perpendicular bisector of the diagonal as you drag the quadrilateral into different configurations?

The Tool Folder

The Tool Folder is a special folder in which you can store frequently used tools. When Sketchpad starts, it checks the Tool Folder and puts every tool in this folder into the Custom Tools menu that appears when you press and hold the **Custom** tools icon.

Creating a Tool Folder

You can create a folder in which you store documents containing frequently used tools. These tools will be available each time you use Sketchpad.

1. Locate the folder the Sketchpad program is located in.
2. If there is no folder named **Tool Folder** within the folder containing Sketchpad, create a new folder.
3. Name this new folder **Tool Folder**.

You can now use this folder to store Sketchpad documents containing frequently used tools. The tools will be available the next time you start Sketchpad.

Storing a Tool in the Tool Folder

To store a tool in the Tool Folder:

You can copy tools between open documents with **Tool Options.**

1. Create or copy the tool(s) you want into a new document.
2. Choose **Save As** from the File menu.
3. Use the Save As dialog box to navigate to the folder named **Tool Folder** located within the same folder which contains the Sketchpad program.
4. Save the document in the Tool Folder.

Alternately, you can drag Sketchpad documents into this folder from your computer's desktop to make their tools available the next time you start Sketchpad.

The new tool will be available the next time you start Sketchpad.

See also: Overview of Custom Tools (p. 90), Using a Custom Tool (p. 92), Custom Tools Menu (p. 91)

Menu Reference

This section describes the commands in Sketchpad's menus. Use the File menu to create, save, and print entire documents. The Edit and Display menus contain commands that alter the appearance, format, or definition of existing objects in your active sketch. The Construct, Transform, Measure, and Graph menus all allow you to define new mathematical content in the active sketch, most often by expressing new objects' relationships to existing, selected objects. The Windows menu (Microsoft Windows only) lets you rearrange open documents on your desktop, and the Help menu allows you to consult an electronic version of this *Reference Manual* for help with specific Sketchpad commands and tools. Finally, the Context menu appears when you right-click (Windows) or Ctrl+click (Macintosh) in the sketch, and presents options relevant to the object that was clicked.

File Menu

This menu contains commands for opening, saving, printing, and otherwise working with Sketchpad documents. Many of these commands are standard commands that appear in most software applications. This chapter briefly describes the familiar aspects of these commands and provides more detail on ways in which Sketchpad treats them differently. If you are unfamiliar with any of the basic commands, you'll probably want to start by looking in the manual that came with your computer.

File	
New Sketch	⌘N
Open...	⌘O
Save	⌘S
Save As...	
Close	⌘W
Document Options...	
Page Setup...	
Print Preview...	
Print...	
Quit	⌘Q

New Sketch

The keyboard shortcut for **New Sketch** is Ctrl+N (Windows) or ⌘+N (Mac).

Opens a new, blank document. A new document window appears on top of all other windows and becomes the active window. The new document is untitled until you name it by saving it.

Open...

The keyboard shortcut for **Open** is Ctrl+O (Windows) or ⌘+O (Mac).

Opens one or more previously saved documents.

When you choose **Open** a dialog appears showing a view of your disk.

1. Navigate to the folder containing your document(s).

2. Click on a name to highlight the document you wish to open.

3. Hold down the Shift key (Macintosh) or Ctrl key (Windows) while clicking additional document names to open more than one document at a time.

4. Click **Open** or double-click the name of the document.

The chosen documents open on your desktop.

Save

The keyboard
shortcut for **Save** is
Ctrl+S (Windows) or
⌘+S (Mac).

Saves whatever changes have been made to the current document since the last time it was saved. If the document is being saved for the first time, the **Save** command prompts you for the location in which to save (see **Save As** below). This command is enabled only if you've made changes in the document since the last time you saved it.

Save As...

Mac users: When first saving a document, Sketchpad suggests a filename ending with the extension **.gsp**. While Macintosh doesn't require file extensions, naming Sketchpad documents with this extension makes it easier to share them with Microsoft Windows users or users on the Internet.

Names and saves the active document in a location that you specify.

When you choose **Save As**, a dialog box like the one at right appears.

1. Navigate your folders to locate the folder in which you want to save your document, or create a new folder, if needed.

2. Type a name for the document.

3. Click **Save**.

Saving Different Copies of a Document

You can use **Save As** to save an additional copy of a previously saved document, with or without changes. For example, imagine you have a document called **Pythag.gsp** to which you want to add action buttons, but you also want to keep a copy of the original version. Make sure you've saved the sketch in the original form, then make the changes and choose **Save As**. Enter a different name for the modified version, such as **Pythag2.gsp**. Now you'll have both versions saved as separate documents.

Saving in Cassiopeia™ Sketchpad Format

You can use **Save As** to save a copy of your document in a form that can be used with the version of Sketchpad available for Casio's Cassiopeia Computer Extender handheld computer. Use the Format (Macintosh) or Save As Type (Windows) menu to choose **Cassiopeia Sketchpad Document** before you click the Save button.

Saving in HTML/JavaSketchpad Format

You can use **Save As** to save a copy of your document in a form that can be used on the World Wide Web with JavaSketchpad. Use the Format (Macintosh) or Save As Type (Windows) menu to choose **HTML/Java Sketchpad Document** before you click the Save button.

See also: JavaSketchpad (p. 226)

Close

The keyboard shortcut for **Close** is Ctrl+W (Windows) or ⌘+W (Mac). You can also use Ctrl+F4 in Windows.

Closes the current document window. You'll be prompted to save any changes you've made since you last saved. The **Close** command does the same thing as clicking the Close box in the upper-left-hand (Mac) or upper-right-hand (Windows) corner of the window's title bar. **Close** does not quit Sketchpad itself.

Document Options...

Manages the pages and custom tools contained in a document. A Sketchpad document can contain multiple pages; use this command to add, remove, rename, and reorder the pages. Similarly, a Sketchpad document can contain multiple custom tools; use the **Document Options** command to copy, remove, rename, and reorder them.

See also: Document Pages (p. 6), Document Tools (p. 7)

View Pages/Tools

Click Pages to manage the pages in your document, or click Tools to manage the custom tools.

List of Pages/Tools

When you're viewing pages, click the name of a page in the list to display that page in the document.

This list shows all the pages or tools in the current document. You can perform the following actions directly on the list items:

- Click on a page or tool in the list, then change its name. (See Page Name/Tool Name.)

- Press and drag a page or tool in the list to change the position of that page or tool in your document.

- Double-click on a page name to display that page and close the dialog box.

Page Name/Tool Name

To rename a page or tool, type a new name here for the page or tool that is chosen in the list box.

Add Page

When you're viewing pages, you can use this pop-up menu to add new pages to your document. Choose **Blank Page** to add a new blank page to your document. Choose from the **Duplicate** submenu to add a duplicate copy of a page from any open document. The top part of the **Duplicate** submenu lists pages from the current document. Listed below a divider are any other open documents; these serve as submenus from which you can choose pages to duplicate and add to the current document.

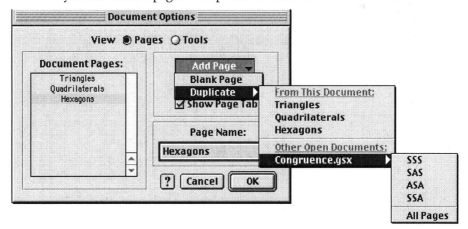

Show Page Tabs

When page tabs aren't showing, Link buttons and the Document Options dialog box are the only ways to move from page to page in your document.

This checkbox appears only when you view page options, not when you view tool options. When Show Page Tabs is checked, tabs appear along the bottom left of the document, showing the names or numbers of the pages. You can use these tabs to navigate among the pages of a document.

Moving the divider at the left edge of a document's horizontal scroll bar all the way to the left has the same effect as unchecking Show Page Tabs. Moving the divider away from the left edge of the window has the same effect as checking Show Page Tabs.

See also: Document Pages (p. 6), Link Buttons (p. 36)

Show Script View

This checkbox appears only when you view tool options, not when you view page options. Check or uncheck this box to show or hide the script view of the most-recently chosen custom tool. The script view allows you to see the given objects and the steps of the tool, to change the properties of the steps, and to observe and control the tool as it functions.

See also: Script View (p. 57)

Copy Tool

Tools that you use frequently and not just in one document can be stored in the Tool Folder. These tools are always available whenever you're using Sketchpad. See p. 98 for information on setting up and using a Tool Folder.

When you're viewing tools, you can use this pop-up menu to copy tools into the active document from other open documents or from documents in your Tool Folder. The top part of the Copy Tool menu lists any other open documents that contain tools; each item provides a submenu from which you can choose a tool to copy and add to the current document. The bottom part of the Copy Tool menu allows you to copy tools from Sketchpad documents into your Tool Folder.

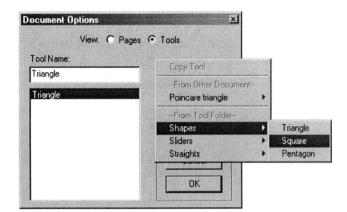

Remove Page/Tool

Before removing a tool or page from your document, you may want to save the document with a different name in order to preserve a copy of that page or tool in case you want it later.

Use this button to permanently remove a page or tool from a document. First choose from the list box the page or tool you wish to remove, then click Remove Page or Remove Tool. Every document must have at least one page, so you cannot remove the only page from a one-page document.

Once you remove a tool or page and click OK, it's gone for good—you cannot get it back. If you decide you don't really want to remove that tool or page, you must click Cancel rather than OK in order to leave your document unchanged.

Page Setup...

Sets up the page size, orientation, and other printing options for your document. This dialog box differs depending on the printer you've chosen as your default printer. To set your default printer, use the Chooser from the Apple menu (Macintosh) or **Settings | Printers** from the Start menu (Windows).

Print Preview...

Displays a preview of your document as it will appear when printed. This dialog box allows you to change the scale of your printout. If the printout will be more than a single sheet of paper, you can view the different sheets to decide which ones to print.

Print...

Prints the current page of the active document on the default printer. The Print dialog box allows you to specify which sheets to print and allows you to print multiple copies. Depending on your printer and operating system, it may also allow you to change printers, decide between color and black-and-white, save output as Postscript, and make other adjustments.

Quit

The keyboard shortcut for **Quit** is Ctrl+Q (Windows) or ⌘+Q (Mac).

Closes all open documents and exits Sketchpad. You'll be prompted to save any unsaved work in open documents before Sketchpad quits.

Edit Menu

The Edit menu contains commands for undoing and redoing recent operations, for managing the clipboard, for creating action buttons, for selecting objects in your sketch, and for modifying various elements and properties of your sketch and of Sketchpad itself.

Edit	
Undo	Ctrl+Z
Redo	Ctrl+R
Cut	Ctrl+X
Copy	Ctrl+C
Paste	Ctrl+V
Clear	Del
Action Buttons	▶
Select All	Ctrl+A
Select Parents	Ctrl+U
Select Children	Ctrl+D
Split/Merge	
Edit Definition...	Ctrl+E
Properties...	Alt+?
Preferences...	

Undo

The keyboard shortcut for **Undo** is Ctrl+Z (Windows) or ⌘+Z (Mac).

This command undoes the most recently performed action.

Use this command in combination with **Redo** to move backward and forward through your recent Sketchpad actions. Sketchpad's capability to undo/redo is unlimited: you can use it to undo your actions, one at a time, all the way back to the point at which you created or opened the sketch. Similarly, after undoing, you can redo those actions to restore your sketch to the state it was in before you started undoing.

Unlimited undo/redo is helpful for correcting mistakes—undoing something you didn't mean to do—or for going back and trying a different approach to a construction—testing a different hypothesis. Unlimited undo is also a way to review your work or someone else's work step-by-step: **Undo** back to the beginning, then **Redo** one step at a time to review each action.

You can undo many steps quickly by repeatedly pressing the keyboard shortcut for **Undo**, or you can undo back to the beginning with only one action by holding down the Shift key, then choosing **Undo**. When you hold down the Shift key, the command becomes **Undo All**.

Undo and **Redo** only apply to geometrically significant actions: They don't apply to formatting changes such as changing labels, text styles, fonts, colors, and line widths.

See also: Redo (p. 110)

Redo

The keyboard shortcut for **Redo** is Ctrl+R (Windows) or ⌘+R (Mac).

This command redoes an action you have undone. If you've undone several steps, you can redo each of those steps.

Redo is available only immediately after using **Undo**. If you take any other action after undoing operations, you can no longer redo the original operations.

Use **Redo** in combination with **Undo** to move backward and forward through your recent Sketchpad actions.

When you hold down the Shift key, **Redo** becomes **Redo All** and redoes all previously undone actions.

Cut

The keyboard shortcut for **Cut** is Ctrl+X (Windows) or ⌘+X (Mac).

This command removes from the sketch any object that is selected, along with any objects that depend on it. Each removed object is placed on the clipboard and can be pasted into the same or a different sketch, or as a picture into another application.

See also: Copy (p. 110), Paste (p. 110), Clear (p. 111), Advanced Graphics Export (p. 223)

Copy

The keyboard shortcut for **Copy** is Ctrl+C (Windows) or ⌘+C (Mac).

This command places a copy of each selected object on the clipboard. The contents of the clipboard can then be pasted into the same or a different sketch, or into another application.

If you're editing a caption or other text, **Copy** puts the selected text on the clipboard. It can then be pasted back into the same or a different sketch, or into another application.

See also: Cut (p. 109), Paste (p. 110), Advanced Graphics Export (p. 223)

Paste

The keyboard shortcut for **Paste** is Ctrl+V (Windows) or ⌘+V (Mac).

This command pastes the contents of the clipboard into the active sketch. If the clipboard contains sketch objects, these objects are inserted into the sketch.

If the clipboard contains a picture, the picture is inserted into the sketch. When you paste a picture, if you have either one or two points selected, the picture's corners will be attached to those points.

If the clipboard contains text and you're editing a caption or other text, the text from the clipboard is inserted into the text you're editing.

See also: Cut (p. 110), Copy (p. 109)

Clear

Pressing the Delete or Backspace key performs the same action as choosing **Clear** from the Edit menu.

This command removes from the sketch any selected object, as well as any objects which depend on it. The removed objects are not placed on the clipboard.

Removing objects from a sketch using **Cut** or **Clear** is very different from hiding them using the **Hide** command. The **Hide** command hides objects from view, but they still exist as part of the sketch. Hidden objects can later be shown, and they continue to affect the behavior of objects that depend on them. Use **Hide** if you want to remove objects from view while maintaining their geometric role in your document; use **Clear**, **Cut**, or **Undo** if you want to remove them permanently from your construction.

See also: Cut (p. 109), Hide Objects (p. 146)

Action Buttons

Action buttons are sketch objects that, when pressed, perform a previously defined action, such as starting an animation or hiding a group of objects.

Each command on the Action Buttons submenu creates a particular kind of action button. Most of these commands display a Properties dialog box panel that allows you to specify how the button you've just created works.

Most action buttons provide a simple way of performing or repeating a common Sketchpad action or activity. For example, you can hide a group of objects by selecting each object in the group and then choosing **Hide Objects** from the Display menu—or you can create a

Hide/Show button that hides or shows the entire group of objects with a single click. You can drag point *A* toward point *B* using the **Arrow** tool—or you can create a Movement button to do it for you. In general, you'll create action buttons for commonly repeated actions for your own convenience and to help communicate about—and present—your sketch to others who may work with it later.

See also: Action Buttons (p. 35), Hide/Show Button (p. 112), Animation Button (p. 112), Movement Button (p. 113), Presentation Button (p. 113), Link Button (p. 113), Scroll Button (p. 114), Arrow Tool (p. 70), Text Tool (p. 86)

Hide/Show Button

This command is available only when at least one object is selected.

Hide Point

Show Objects

It creates a button that hides or shows each selected object. Normally the button's label changes from *Hide* to *Show* depending on whether the objects it controls are visible or not. (When some objects are visible and some are not, the button is labeled *Hide*.)

You can use the Hide/Show panel of **Properties** to change various aspects of the button's behavior. For example, you can make the button always show its objects or always hide its objects, instead of toggling between hiding and showing. You can also use this panel to prevent the button from selecting its objects after showing them or to make it show or hide its objects instantly instead of fading them in or out.

See also: Action Buttons (p. 35), Hide/Show Properties (p. 125)

Animation Button

This command is available only when at least one selected object can be animated. (Only geometric objects and parameters can be animated.)

Animate Point

It creates a button that animates each selected object. Sketchpad animates independent points freely in the plane. Points constructed on objects are animated along the objects on which they're constructed; other geometric objects are animated by animating each point on which they depend. And finally, numeric parameters are animated by changing their numeric value.

You may want to familiarize yourself with the basic **Animate** command from the Display menu before creating action buttons to perform animations for you.

When you create an Animation button, the Animate panel of the Properties dialog box appears, allowing you to set the speed and direction for each animated point and for each animated parameter.

Click the button once to start the animation; the button remains pressed until the animation is finished. You can click the button a second time, while the button is still pressed, to stop the animation.

See also: Animate (p. 150), Action Buttons (p. 35), Animate Properties (p. 127)

Movement Button

This command is available only when the selection contains at least one pair of points. (You must have selected an even number of points.)

`Move A -> B`

After creating a Movement button, you may want to hide the *destination* points so only the *moving* points are visible.

It creates a button that moves the first point of each selected pair toward the second. You can select as many pairs of points as you want; the first point of each pair (the *moving* point) always moves toward the second (the *destination* point).

When you create a Movement button, the Move panel of the Properties dialog box appears, allowing you to set the speed and characteristics of the motion.

Click the button once to start the movement; the button remains pressed until all moving points reach their destinations. You can click the button a second time, while the button is still pressed, to stop the movement.

See also: Animate (p. 150), Action Buttons (p. 35), Move Properties (p. 129)

Presentation Button

This command is available only when at least one action button is selected.

`Present 2 Actions`

It creates a button that activates the selected buttons' actions either simultaneously or sequentially to form a presentation. Pressing a Presentation button has the same effect as pressing each of its selected parent actions either all at once or one after the other. Use Presentation buttons when you want to combine several related actions into a single button for ease of use.

When you create a Presentation button, the Presentation panel of the Properties dialog box appears, allowing you to specify whether to present the selected actions simultaneously or sequentially, as well as to set other properties of the Presentation.

See also: Action Buttons (p. 35), Properties (p. 120), Presentation Properties (p. 130), Object Relationships: Parents and Children (p. 10)

Link Button

Use **Document Options** from the File menu to add multiple pages to your document.

This command creates a button that links to a different page of the document or that links to an Internet URL such as a remote web site.

When you create a Link button, the Link panel of the Properties dialog box appears, allowing you to determine whether the button links to a different document page or to a URL. If the button links to a document page, you can also specify an action button on that page that will be activated when the link occurs.

Use URLs to connect your sketch to related mathematical, historic, or reference material available on the Internet.

See also: Action Buttons (p. 35), Properties (p. 120), Link Properties (p. 130), Document Options (p. 104)

Scroll Button

This command is available only when a single point is selected.

It creates a button that scrolls the window based on the position of the selected point.

Use Scroll buttons when you want to be able to "jump" to a point anywhere in the scrollable plane.

When you create a Scroll button, the Scroll panel of the Properties dialog box appears to allow you to determine whether the button scrolls the window to put the selected point at the top left corner of the window, or to put the selected point in the center of the window.

See also: Action Buttons (p. 35), Properties (p. 120), Scroll Properties (p. 133)

Select All

The keyboard shortcut for **Select All** is Ctrl+A (Windows) or ⌘+A (Mac).

This command selects all objects that match the active tool in the Toolbox.

If a **Selection Arrow** or **Custom** tool is active, this command selects all objects in the sketch.

If another tool from the Toolbox is active (**Point, Compass, Segment, Ray, Line,** or **Text**), all matching objects are selected. For example, if the **Ray** tool is active, the command becomes **Select All Rays**.

See also: Select Parents (p. 115), Select Children (p. 115), Object Relationships: Parents and Children (p. 10)

Select Parents

The keyboard shortcut for **Select Parents** is Ctrl+U (Windows) or ⌘+U (Mac). (Think "<u>U</u>p the family tree.")

This command selects the parents of each selected object.

The *parents* of an object are those objects upon which the object directly depends. For example, a segment's parents are the endpoints used to define it; a midpoint's parent is the segment on which it's constructed.

If the selected object has no parents (in other words, if it's an *independent* object), it remains selected. If the parents of the selected object are hidden, the selected object is deselected (leaving nothing selected).

See also: Select All (p. 114), Select Children (p. 115), Object Relationships: Parents and Children (p. 10)

Select Children

The keyboard shortcut for **Select Children** is Ctrl+D (Windows) or ⌘+D (Mac). (Think "<u>D</u>own the family tree.")

This command selects the children of each selected object.

The *children* of an object are those objects that directly depend on the object. For example, a circle constructed by the **Circle By Center+Radius** command is a child of both the point and the segment used to define it.

If the selected object has no children, it remains selected. If the children of the selected object are hidden, the selected object is deselected (leaving nothing selected).

See also: Select All (p. 114), Select Parents (p. 115), Object Relationships: Parents and Children (p. 10)

Split/Merge

The **Split** and **Merge** commands allow you to alter the relationships of existing objects by splitting points from their parents, by merging points either with other points or onto paths, and by merging several text objects into one. These commands allow you to fix construction mistakes, to make significant changes in a sketch without starting over, and to modify geometric and mathematical investigations in flexible and powerful ways.

Splitting a Point from Its Parent

When you select a single midpoint, a point on a path, or a point of intersection, the command becomes **Split Midpoint From Segment, Split Intersection From Path Objects,** or something similar. If the selected point is a point on path, it's removed from its path. If the selected point is an intersection point, it's split from the intersecting objects. In either case, it becomes an independent point and can be dragged anywhere.

Split Point From Circle

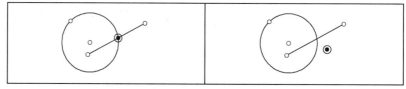

Split Intersection From Path Objects

Splitting a Point Apart

In this example, if you want to split the circle center from the segment endpoint while leaving the two segments with a common endpoint, first split the point apart, then select the two segment endpoints and choose **Merge Points**.

An independent point with more than one child can be split into multiple points, one for each child. For example, a point that is the center of a circle and is also the endpoint of two segments can be split so that the circle center and segment endpoints are now three separate, unrelated points. Select the point you wish to split and choose **Split Point** from the Edit menu. The point splits into two or more separate points a small distance from each other.

To split a point apart, you must select an independent point with two or more children.

Split Point

Merging Two Points

Merging two points is a handy way to fix any mistakes you make while using drawing tools.

Two separate points can be combined into a single point using the **Merge** command. Select an independent point and the point to which you want to merge it. One of the points must be independent so that it's free to merge with the other point. The other point doesn't have to be independent, but it must not depend on the first. (If the second point could depend on the first, after merging, it would be defined in terms of itself!)

Merge Points

Merging a Point to a Path

A point can be merged to a path (straight object, circle, arc, interior, point locus, or function plot) using the **Merge** command. Select an independent point and a path that doesn't depend on that point. The point must be independent, and the path must not be dependent on the point. In this way, for example, an endpoint of a segment can be joined or merged to another segment. After it's merged, the point is attached to the segment and can move along the segment but cannot leave it (unless you **Split** it from that segment).

Merge Point To Segment

Merging Text

You can merge separate text elements—where at least one is a caption—into a single "sentence." For example, you can merge a caption and two measurements together to read "The model is 5.2 cm tall and 3.1 cm wide." Select the text you wish to merge (captions, measurements, or labeled objects) in the order you wish it read and choose **Merge Text** from the Edit menu. Sketchpad consolidates the separate pieces of text into a single caption. The resulting composite caption includes the text of selected captions, the labels of selected labeled objects, and the values of selected measurements and calculations. The order in which the objects were selected determines the order in which they appear in the final composite caption.

Splitting Merged Text

To return a single merged caption to its component parts, select the merged caption and choose **Split Merged Text** from the Edit menu. Sketchpad splits the caption back into the parts you originally merged.

2. m $\overline{AB}$ = 5.2 cm		m$\overline{AB}$ = 5.2 cm
4. m $\overline{AC}$ = 3.1 cm		m$\overline{AC}$ = 3.1 cm
1. The model is $\rightarrow$ The model is 5.2 cm tall and 3.1 cm wide! $\rightarrow$	The model is	
3. tall and		tall and
5. wide!		wide!

Select the text objects in the order shown at left and choose **Merge Text** to create the center caption. Select the merged text and choose **Split Merged Text** to return the individual elements to their original positions (right).

See also: Object Paths (p. 13), How to Use Split and Merge to Explore Constructions (p. 118), Object Relationships: Parents and Children (p. 10), Composite Captions (p. 34)

How To . . . Use **Split** and **Merge** to Explore Constructions

The **Split** and **Merge** commands are often useful when you're investigating the behavior of a particular construction and you want to see what happens in the case of a slightly different construction. In this extended example, you'll construct the diagonals of a general quadrilateral, then investigate what happens when you turn the quadrilateral into a parallelogram, a rectangle, or a rhombus.

To begin, construct quadrilateral *ABCD*, its two diagonals, and the point of intersection *E* of the diagonals. Then measure the distances and angle shown in the figure at right. Drag the vertices around to see if there's any relationship between the various measurements.

EA = 2.25 cm   EC = 1.52 cm
EB = 2.40 cm   ED = 0.81 cm
m∠AEB = 100°

Now turn the quadrilateral into a parallelogram. Construct two parallel lines as shown at right: one through *D* parallel to the segment from *A* to *B* and another through *B* parallel to the segment from *A* to *D*. Also construct the intersection of the parallels.

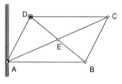

Select both point *C* and the intersection, and choose **Merge Points** to merge the vertex with the intersection point.

Hide the parallel lines. Then drag vertices *A*, *B*, and *D*. How are the measurements now related?

Next turn the quadrilateral into a rectangle by making ∠*BAD* into a right angle. Construct a perpendicular as shown at right and **Merge** point *D* to the perpendicular. Again, drag the vertices and watch the measurements. Do you notice anything different?

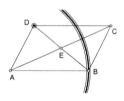

Finally, change your quadrilateral into a rhombus. First **Split** *D* from the perpendicular. Then construct a circle centered at *A* and passing through *B*, and **Merge** *D* to the circle. Drag the vertices once more to see what relationships the measurements now reveal.

Edit Definition

Editing definitions allows you not only to correct any mistakes you might make, but also to explore a mathematical model over an unlimited range of cases.

This command allows you to edit the definition of a selected calculation, function, numeric parameter, or plotted point. If you select a parameter, a calculation or a function, the Calculator appears, allowing you to modify the value or expression. If you select a plotted point, the Plot Points dialog box appears, allowing you to change the point's coordinates.

This command's name changes to match the selected object.

Select:	For this command:
One calculation	**Edit Calculation**
One function	**Edit Function**
One parameter	**Edit Parameter**
One plotted point	**Edit Plotted Point**

You can also double-click any of these objects with the **Arrow** tool as a shortcut for **Edit Definition**.

See also: Calculator (p. 47), New Parameter (p. 202), Calculate (p. 194), New Function (p. 202), Plot Points (p. 201)

Properties

The keyboard shortcut for **Properties** is Alt+? (Windows) or ⌘+? (Mac).

This command allows you to change a variety of properties of a single selected object. Select one object and choose **Properties** from the Edit menu to display a dialog box that allows you to alter the object's properties.

As an alternative, you can use the Context menu to access **Properties**. In Windows, right-click on the object. On a Mac, hold down the Ctrl key while you click on the object. **Properties** is the command that appears directly under your mouse in the resulting Context menu.

The Properties dialog box is arranged into separate panels of related properties. Switch from panel to panel by clicking on the tabs near the top of the dialog box. Which panels are available depends on the type of object selected.

While you're modifying one object's properties, you can switch to a different object by clicking on that object in the sketch. (If the object to which you want to switch is obscured by the Properties dialog box, you'll first have to move the Properties dialog box aside to reveal the object.)

When you finish modifying an object's properties, click OK to make the changes permanent or click Cancel to leave the object with its original properties. When you click in the sketch to switch to a different object, your changes for the original object are made permanent before Sketchpad switches to the new object, just as if you'd clicked OK for that original object.

Keep in mind that for any specific object, only a few panels appear—not all of them!

The following sections describe all of the possible Property panels, as well as the types of object for which each panel appears.

See also: Objects (p. 8), Context Menu (p. 207)

Object Properties

All objects have an Object Properties panel. In the panel, the object's geometric definition is described, usually in terms of its relation to its parents (the objects that geometrically define the object).

Use the Parents and Children menus to navigate the family tree—that is, to find an object's ancestors or descendants. This is a good way to learn how a particular object was constructed, to locate a particular object in a complicated sketch, or to display one particular hidden object.

Q: If an object is no longer arrow-selectable, how do you select it again to change its properties back to being arrow-selectable?
A: Click it with the right mouse button (in Windows), or hold down the Ctrl key (Mac) to access **Properties** via the Context menu.

Parents, Children: Click on either the Parents or Children pop-up menu to see the parents or children of the current object. As you move through either of these lists, the corresponding object in the sketch is highlighted.

Choose an object from either the Parent or Child pop-up list to switch to showing the properties of this related object. When you switch to a different object in this way, any changes you've made in the properties of the original object become permanent.

Hidden: Use this checkbox to determine whether the object is hidden or visible.

Arrow Selectable: Use this checkbox to determine whether the object can be selected by clicking on it with the **Arrow** tool. Normally, you'll leave this property checked. If you clear the check-box, the object will no longer be selected when clicked by the **Arrow** tool or when you use the selection rectangle. This can be handy when you're working with something like a pasted picture that you want to use as the backdrop of a geometric measurement activity. You don't want to accidentally select and drag this picture while working "on top" of it, so you may wish to make it not arrow-selectable.

See also: Hide Objects (p. 146), Show All Hidden (p. 146), Object Relationships: Parents and Children (p. 10), Selecting Objects Using a Selection Rectangle (p. 71)

Label Properties

All points, straight objects, arcs, interiors, point loci, function plots, and measurements have a Label panel.

Use the Label panel to change an object's label, to change whether and how the label is displayed, and to change whether the label is used in custom tools.

```
╔══════════════════════════════════════════════╗
║ ═══════ Properties of Point A ═══════         ║
║  ╱Object╲╱Label╲                               ║
║                                                ║
║   Label: │A                              │    ║
║                                                ║
║   ┌────────────────────────────────────┐      ║
║   │ ☑ Show Label                        │      ║
║   │                          ┌────────┐ │      ║
║   │ ☐ Use Label in Custom Tools│ Style...││    ║
║   │                          └────────┘ │      ║
║   └────────────────────────────────────┘      ║
║                    [?] [ Cancel ] [  OK  ]     ║
╚══════════════════════════════════════════════╝
```

If you enter a label that ends in brackets—such as A[1]—the bracketed quantity will display as a subscript in your sketch. In other words, type A[1] in Label Properties to display A_1 in your sketch.

Label: This box displays the label of the selected object. It will be blank if a label has not yet been assigned to the object. Type a new label to change the object's label.

Style: Click on this button to display a dialog box in which you can adjust the font, size, and typeface in which the label is displayed.

Show Label: Use this checkbox to hide or show the object's label. (This checkbox is unavailable for objects that cannot display separate labels, such as measures.)

The final checkbox in Label Properties differs depending on the context. It appears as Use Label in Custom Tools for a sketch object, but for a custom tool object appears as either Automatically Match Sketch Object (for a given) or Use Label in Sketches (for a step).

Use Label in Custom Tools: Use this checkbox to determine whether the label of a sketch object will be used in custom tools. Normally, custom tools assign new and unique labels to the objects they create. So, if you are defining a custom tool that includes an object with a special label—such as "hypotenuse" or "orthocenter"—and you want to duplicate that label whenever the tool is used, you should check this option. This box appears only when viewing properties for a sketch object.

Use Label in Sketches: Use this checkbox to determine whether or not the label of a custom tool step object will be used in sketches. With this box unchecked, the custom tool assigns a new and unique label when it constructs this step. When the box is checked, the step's label is used whenever a sketch object is constructed from this step. This box appears only when using the Script View to view properties of a custom tool step object.

To view the properties of a custom tool object, you must make that tool the chosen tool, and choose Show Script View from the Custom Tools menu.

Automatically Match Sketch Object: Use this checkbox to determine whether or not a custom tool given object will be automatically matched to an object with the same label in the sketch. This box appears only when using the Script View to view properties of a custom tool given object. When this box is checked, the object appears in Script View as an assumed given. When not checked, the object apepars in Script View as a normal given.

See also: Text Tool (p. 86), Text Palette (p. 53), Custom Tools (p. 90), Show Script View (p. 96), Advanced Tool Topics (p. 220), Custom Tools Menu (p. 91)

Value Properties

Measurements, calculations, and parameters have a Value panel. Use this panel to set the precision and the display name of these objects and to set the value of parameter objects.

Properties of Parameter t[1]

Object | Label | Value | Parameter

Precision
hundredths

Display With
○ Original Name   ○ No Name   ● Current Label

Parameter
Value: 1.0

Help   Cancel   OK

Precision: In this box you can set the precision with which the measurement is displayed. Choices range from units to hundred-thousandths. This setting determines only what Sketchpad rounds the value to when the value is displayed on-screen; Sketchpad normally stores the actual value with considerably more accuracy, and this setting doesn't cause any loss of accuracy in the value Sketchpad uses internally.

Display With: Use this to set the on-screen name that will appear before the value. For instance, if you've measured the length of the segment from A to B and changed the measurement's label to *Length,* the three possible ways to display the value are illustrated here.

Original Name:	m $\overline{AB}$ = 4.00 cm
No Name:	4.00 cm
Current Label:	Length = 4.00 cm

You can also choose **Edit Parameter** from the Edit menu or double-click with the **Arrow** tool to change a parameter's value.

Parameter: In this box you can set the value of a parameter. (This is available only for parameters, not for measurements and other calculations.)

See also: Measurements, Calculations, and Parameters (p. 18), Edit Parameter Definition (p. 119), Accuracy vs. Precision (p. 136)

Plot Properties

The default number of samples assigned to newly constructed loci and function plots is determined by Sampling Preferences.

Only loci and functions have a Plot panel. Both panels allow you to set the number of samples used to plot the locus or function. The greater the number of samples, the smoother and more accurate the plot is. However, the greater the number of samples, the slower Sketchpad can be in calculating and displaying the plot.

Plot Properties for a Locus

You can adjust the number of samples in a locus or function plot without going to Properties by selecting the sampled object and pressing the + or – key while your sketch window is active.

Use this panel to set the number of samples in a locus. If the locus is a point locus, you can also use this panel to determine whether the locus is displayed in continuous or discrete form. The illustration that follows shows an elliptical point locus displayed in continuous form on the left and in discrete form on the right.

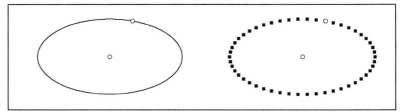

Plot Properties for a Function Plot

You can also set the domain of a plotted function by dragging the arrowheads that appear at the endpoints of the function plot.

When entering limits for the domain, you can use mathematical expressions like 2*3 and π/4. (Windows users: Press p for π. Mac users: Press Option+p.)

Use this panel to set the domain of a plotted function, to set the number of samples used to display the function, and to determine whether the function plot is displayed in continuous or discrete form. By default, Sketchpad plots new functions over a domain corresponding to the width of the screen.

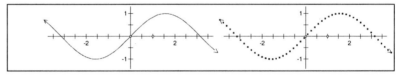

The illustration that follows shows a function plot displayed in continuous form on the left and in discrete form on the right.

See also: Loci (p. 24), Functions and Function Plots (p. 27), Sampling Preferences (p. 139)

Parameter Properties

Use this panel to change the default animation behavior of a parameter. The settings on this panel determine how the parameter's value changes when you select the parameter and either press the + or − key to change the value manually or choose **Animate** from the Display menu. These settings are also used as the initial settings when you create an Animation button that animates the parameter.

Continuously/Discretely: Check the Discretely radio button to make the parameter's value jump by the amount in the units box each time it changes. Check Continuously to make the value change gradually instead of by jumps.

units per sec: The numbers here determine how quickly the parameter's value changes. This rate is not exact; if your computer is very busy doing other tasks, the parameter may change more slowly than the rate you specify here.

Domain: These numbers determine the minimum and maximum values of the parameter during animation. You can still change the value directly (by double-clicking with the **Arrow** tool or by choosing **Edit Parameter** from the Display menu) to any value you like, no matter what these domain limits are.

Keyboard (+/−) Adjustments: This number specifies the amount by which the parameter changes when you select it and press the + or − key on the keyboard.

See also: Measurements, Calculations, and Parameters (p. 18), Animation Button (p. 112), New Parameter (p. 202), Edit Parameter Definition (p. 119), Animate (p. 150)

Hide/Show Properties

This panel appears only for Hide/Show action buttons. Use it to determine the type of action the Hide/Show button performs as well as various aspects of how it works.

If you don't change the default label of a toggling Hide/Show button, the label changes between Hide and Show to describe the action it will perform next.

Action: Choose Always Show Objects to make this button into a Show button, which always shows the objects to which it applies. Choose Always Hide Objects to make this button into a Hide button, which always hides the objects to which it applies. Choose Toggle Between Hide and Show to make this a toggling Hide/Show button, which hides objects when clicked on if one or more of its objects are showing and shows its objects when clicked on if they are all hidden.

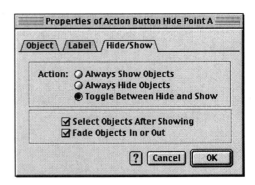

Effects: If Select Objects After Showing is checked, when you click on a Show button all its parental objects are selected. (Even if some of the button's objects are already showing, they are still selected.) If unchecked, the objects are left unselected after they're shown.

If Fade Objects In or Out is checked, objects fade in or out of visibility gradually when you click on the Hide/Show button. If unchecked, objects appear or disappear immediately.

See also: Action Buttons (p. 35), Hide/Show Button (p. 112), Hide Objects (p. 146), Show All Hidden (p. 146), Object Relationships: Parents and Children (p. 10)

Animate Properties

This panel appears only for Animation action buttons. Use it to determine how each animated object moves.

The list at the top describes the motion of each animated object. If the button animates an object that can move only by moving its parents, the list shows the parents rather than the object itself. (For instance, if you animate the segment from point *A* to point *B*, the list shows *A* and *B* rather than the segment.) When you highlight an object in the list, the details of that object's animation settings appear in the lower part of the panel, and you can modify the settings to change how the animation works.

Animating points or parameters randomly is particularly useful for investigations in probability, statistics and chaos.

Direction: For parameters and for points that are animated on paths, you can set the direction of the motion. The available choices depend on the kind of path and the kind of objects. For instance, if the path is a circle or circle interior, the first two choices are counter-clockwise and clockwise. If the path is a straight object, arc, or polygon interior, the first two choices are forward and backward. If the animated object is a parameter, the first two choices are increasing and decreasing.

If you choose random direction for a point on a path, the point moves to a new randomly chosen position on its path each time it moves. Similarly, if you choose random direction for a parameter, the parameter takes on a new random value within its domain each time it moves.

The Once Only check box is not available when a point or parameter is moving bidirectionally.

Once Only: For a parameter or a point on a path which is moving randomly, you can check Once Only to stop the animation after it generates a single new random position or value. For points on paths that aren't moving randomly, you can check Once Only to stop the animation when the point returns to its starting position. For parameters which aren't moving randomly, you can check Once Only to stop the animation when the parameter returns to its starting value.

Speed: This portion of the dialog box appears only for points, and allows you to set the speed of an animated point to slow, medium, fast, or some other desired value.

The rate at which a parameter changes its value is not exact. Sketchpad tries to change the value at the designated rate, but if your computer is busy with other tasks, the parameter may change more slowly than the rate set here.

Change Value: This portion of the dialog box appears only for parameters, and allows you to determine how a parameter's value changes. You can determine whether the value changes continuously or discretely (jumping by an increment you set each time the value changes). You can determine how quickly the value changes, and the domain within which the value can vary.

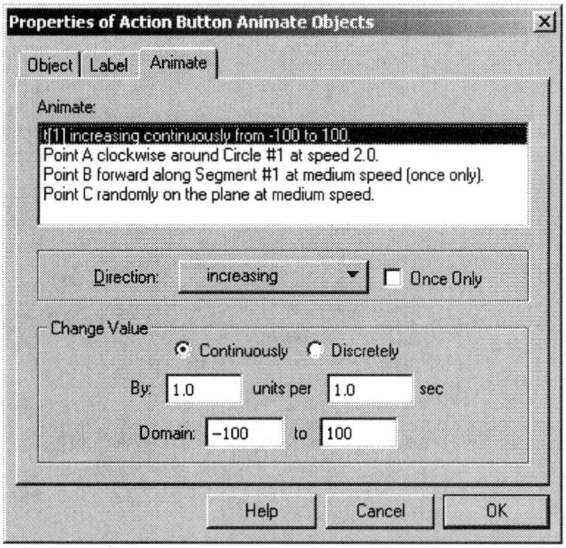

Properties of Action Button Animate Objects ☒

Object | Label | Animate |

Animate:

> t[1] increasing continuously from -100 to 100.
> Point A clockwise around Circle #1 at speed 2.0.
> Point B forward along Segment #1 at medium speed (once only).
> Point C randomly on the plane at medium speed.

Direction: increasing ▼ ☐ Once Only

Change Value
⦿ Continuously ⦾ Discretely

By: 1.0 units per 1.0 sec

Domain: -100 to 100

Help | Cancel | OK

See also: Animation Buttons (p. 112), Animate (p. 150), Measurements, Calculations, and Parameters (p. 18), New Parameter (p. 202), Object Relationships: Parents and Children (p. 10)

Move Properties

This panel appears only for Movement action buttons, and allows you to set their speed and behavior.

You can set the movement speed to slow, medium, fast, or instant.

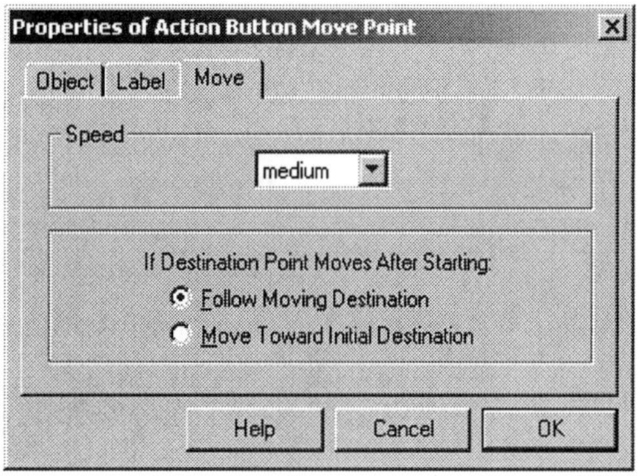

Properties of Action Button Move Point ☒

Object | Label | Move |

Speed
medium ▼

If Destination Point Moves After Starting:
⦿ Follow Moving Destination
⦾ Move Toward Initial Destination

Help | Cancel | OK

If the destination point is moving, it's possible that the moving point will never reach the destination and will keep moving forever. You can take advantage of this "perpetual motion" to model kinematic systems.

If the destination point moves while the Movement button is active, you can decide how the moving point will travel. Choose Follow Moving Destination to have the moving point alter direction as the destination point moves, always continuing to move toward that point. Choose Move Toward Initial Destination to have the moving point travel in a straight line to the location of the destination point at the instant the Movement button was clicked, stopping when it reaches that initial destination.

See also: Action Buttons (p. 35), Movement Button (p. 113)

Presentation Properties

This panel appears only for Presentation action buttons. A Presentation button presents the actions of a set of other parental buttons.

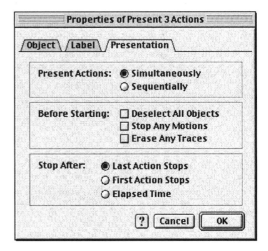

Present Actions: This choice is available only when the Presentation button presents more than one other action. (In other words, it's available when the Presentation has more than one parental action button.)

Choose Simultaneously to activate all actions of the presentation at the same time. Pressing a simultaneous Presentation button has the same effect as activating all of its parental action buttons at once. If you choose Simultaneously, you can also set stopping conditions for the Presentation (see Stop After, below).

When you present a parental Animation button sequentially, Sketchpad waits for the animation to complete before continuing the sequenced presentation. If the animation doesn't complete on its own, you can stop it yourself either by releasing the pressed Animation button, or by choosing **Stop Animation** from the Display menu while the animation is continuing. Once the animation stops, the sequenced presentation resumes.

Choose Sequentially to activate the actions of the presentation one after another in the order in which they were selected when the button was created. Pressing a sequential Presentation button has the same effect as pressing the parental action buttons one at a time, waiting for each activated action to be completed before proceeding to the next parental action. If you choose Sequentially, you can also specify a pause between presented actions (see Pause Between Actions, below).

Before Starting: Check these options to specify any additional effects you'd like to occur at the moment the Presentation button is pressed. Based on your choices, Sketchpad will deselect any previously selected objects, stop any previously started animations, and erase any previously displayed traces before commencing the presentation.

Stop After: This choice is available only when the presentation presents actions simultaneously. When Stop After Last Action Stops is chosen, each of the presented actions is allowed to proceed independently, and the presentation completes only when the last presented action has finished. If you choose Stop After First Action Stops, all of the presented actions stop as soon as the first presented action stops. (This choice can be useful for coordinating two or more animation or movement actions.) When you choose Stop After Elapsed Time, the dialog box allows you to enter an overall duration in seconds for the presented actions. (This choice is useful when you want to stop an animation after a fixed amount of time.)

Pause Between Actions: This choice is available only when the presentation presents actions sequentially. Enter the amount of time (in seconds) you want to pause between each step of the sequence. If you enter zero, each step of the presentation commences as soon as the previous step completes. If you enter a nonzero pause, Sketchpad waits between steps.

See also: Action Buttons (p. 35), Presentation Button (p. 113), Object Relationships: Parents and Children (p. 10)

Link Properties

This panel appears only for Link buttons. Use the Link To radio buttons to choose whether the button links to another page in your document or to an Internet URL such as a web page.

Use the **Document Options** command from the File menu to add or copy new pages into your document.

Page: When this is chosen, the Link button will link to a different page of the current document. Use the Page pop-up menu to decide which page to link to. If that page contains any action buttons of its own (such as an Animation or Movement button), you can choose one of those buttons in the Button On Page pop-up menu to cause the Link button to automatically activate the specified button on the linked page.

The default URL points to the Sketchpad Resource Center, a web site with additional resources and information about using Sketchpad. Copy web page URLs from your browser and paste them here.

URL: When this is chosen, the Link button will link to a URL using your web browser. You must enter the actual URL, which can be a web site (if the URL starts with "http://") or a local file or program (if the URL starts with "file:///").

URL links can also use these two special URL forms:

sketchdoc://: Start the URL with "sketchdoc://" to link to a document in the same folder as the current document. For example, if you want to link from a document named **Demo1.gsx** to a document called **Demo2.gsx** in the same folder, you could use the URL "sketchdoc://Demo2.gsx".

sketchapp://: Start the URL with "sketchapp://" to link to a document in the same folder as the Sketchpad application.

Internet URLs such as http:// web sites are only accessible if you're connected to the Internet and have a web browser installed on your computer, of course. Local file:/// URLs are useful for accessing files or other resources on your specific computer, but these buttons may not function if you open your document on another computer (which may well be missing the linked-to files). The relative URLs—sketchdoc:// and sketchapp://—let you refer to resources in relation to "known locations" on any computer running Sketchpad. They can be handy if you're creating a folder of linked documents you'd like to share with others. As long as you use sketchdoc:// URLs, the documents within that folder will stay linked together no matter where you move or copy that folder.

See also: Action Buttons (p. 35), Link Button (p. 113), Document Options (p. 104)

Scroll Properties

This panel appears only for Scroll action buttons. A Scroll button scrolls the window in which it's located to show a specific portion of that window. The Scroll button is based on a point, and the scrolling action can scroll in one of two ways: so that the parental point is at the top left corner of the window or so that the parental point is centered in the window.

See also: Action Buttons (p. 35), Scroll Button (p. 114), Object Relationships: Parents and Children (p. 10)

Iteration Properties

Only iterated images and iteration rules have an Iteration panel. Use this panel to set the number of iterations, to specify whether the iterations display all levels or only the final iteration, and to determine how random points in the iteration behave.

You can adjust the number of iterations without going to Properties by selecting an iterated image and pressing the + or – key while your sketch window is active.

Number of Iterations: This number determines how many times the iteration is repeated. The minimum value you can use is 1; the maximum value depends on the iteration and is smaller for complex iterations that involve more than a single map. If the number of iterations—the iteration depth—was defined by a measurement or calculated value when the iteration was first created, the current depth is displayed here but cannot be edited.

Display As: Set this to Full Orbit to display all the iterated images (the images for every level of the iteration). Set this to Final Iteration Only to display only the images at the final level, as set by the Number of Iterations.

You can randomize an iteration without going to Properties by selecting an iterated image and pressing the ! key while your sketch window is active.

Move Iterated Points on Objects: This choice appears only for iterations in which one or more of the pre-images are mapped to a point on the path. It determines how iterated images of such points behave. Set this to Same Locations in order to have each iterated image appear in the same relative location on its path as the first image does on its original path. Set this to Random Locations to have each iterated image appear at a random location on its path. When you've set this to Random Locations, the Randomize Now button is enabled; you can click this button to assign each image point on the path a new random position.

See also: Iterations and Iterated Images (p. 31), Iterate (p. 178), Keyboard Reference (p. 209), Parametric Depth (p. 185)

Preferences

Use the Context menu as a shortcut to **Preferences**. Right-click (Windows) or Ctrl+click (Macintosh) in a blank area to invoke the Context menu.

This command allows you to change a variety of settings that determine how Sketchpad works.

The Preferences dialog box normally includes three panels: Units, Color, and Text.

An **Advanced Preferences** command allows you to control additional aspects of Sketchpad's operation that need to be changed rarely, if ever. That command is described in the next section.

If you want some changes to apply only to the current sketch and some to apply only to new sketches, you'll need to open the Preferences dialog box twice.

When you make changes in Sketchpad's Preferences, you can use the checkboxes at the bottom

Apply To: ☑ This Sketch ☐ New Sketches

of the dialog box to decide whether your changes will apply to the current sketch only, to new sketches only, or to both the current sketch and new sketches. Choose Apply To: This Sketch to have your changes affect newly constructed objects in the current sketch. Click Apply To:

New Sketches to have your changes affect all new sketches (including new blank pages you add to the current document).

See also: Units Preferences (p. 135), Color Preferences (p. 136), Text Preferences (p. 137), Advanced Preferences (p. 138), Context Menu (p. 207)

Units Preferences

The unit settings on this panel also affect the units in which you specify angles and distances for translations and rotations in other dialog boxes.

The settings on this panel control the units and precision Sketchpad uses to display measurements and calculations. For example, depending on these settings, a segment's length measurement may appear as "2.54 cm" or "1.0 in."

```
┌──────────────── Preferences ────────────────┐
│ ╱Units╲ ╱Color╲ ╱Text╲                        │
│   ┌─────────────────────────────────────┐    │
│   │              Units      Precision   │    │
│   │   Angle:  [degrees ▼] [hundredths ▼]│    │
│   │ Distance: [cm      ▼] [hundredths ▼]│    │
│   │ Scalars (Slope, Ratio, ...): [hundredths ▼]│ │
│   └─────────────────────────────────────┘    │
│              ☑ This Sketch                    │
│   Apply To:  ☐ New Sketches  [?] [Cancel] [OK]│
└──────────────────────────────────────────────┘
```

The choices for Angle Units are **degrees, directed degrees,** or **radians.**

With *directed* degrees or radians, ∠*ABC* has the opposite measure as ∠*CBA*. With "plain" degrees, both of these angles have the same measure. Directed degrees are useful in transformational geometry, where the *direction* as well as the *magnitude* of an angle is important.

- Measurements in degrees are always positive and range from 0° to 180°.

    C m∠ABC = 20°
    B ──── A m∠CBA = 20°

- Measurements in directed degrees are positive for counter-clockwise angles and negative for clockwise angles. Directed degrees range from –180° to 180°.

    C m∠ABC = 20°
    B ──── A m∠CBA = -20°

- Measures of angles in radians are always directed and range from –π to π.

    C m∠ABC = 0.11π radians
    B ──── A m∠CBA = -0.11π radians

Set the Distance Units to **cm, inches,** or **pixels.** A pixel is a single dot on the computer screen and usually corresponds to about 1/72 inch on Macintosh and 1/96 inch in Windows.

Sketchpad's distance measurements are accurate when printed, but may not be exactly accurate on the screen, depending on the size of your monitor and on the resolution you've set in your computer's control panel. In the event that you require exactly accurate on-screen distance measurements, use the System Preferences panel to set the precise number of pixels per inch or per centimeter on your screen. This panel is available only in **Advanced Preferences.**

The choices for each of the three Precision settings are **units, tenths, hundredths, thousandths, ten-thousandths,** and **hundred-thousandths** (0, 1, 2, 3, 4, and 5 decimal places, respectively). These settings only affect how numbers are displayed, not how they are represented internally.

See also: System Preferences (p. 140), Accuracy vs. Precision (p. 136)

User Tip   Accuracy vs. Precision

Be careful not to confuse accuracy with precision. If you are displaying distances precise to the nearest tenth, Sketchpad can accurately represent the sum of two lengths measuring 1.4 as
`1.4 + 1.4 = 2.8.`
If your precision is set to round displayed values to the nearest unit, however, the sum may seem nonsensical:
`1 + 1 = 3.`

The *accuracy* of a measurement in Sketchpad refers to how close the measured value is to the ideal, "correct" value. The *precision* of a measurement in Sketchpad refers to the number of decimal places used when the value is displayed on the screen.

The accuracy of Sketchpad's measurements and calculations is determined by the full computational power of your computer. Initial computations are usually accurate to about 15 significant digits. For instance, the square root of 2 is stored internally as 1.41421356237310. Calculations based on these initial values may be less accurate, because errors in the accuracy compound across calculations.

The precision of displayed measurements is determined by your choice in Units Preferences. Sketchpad rounds calculated values to your chosen precision when displaying them.

See also: Sketchpad's Internal Mathematics (p. 234)

Color Preferences

The settings on this panel control the updating of color preferences, the default colors of new objects you create, the background and selection colors used in your sketch, and the fading behavior of traces.

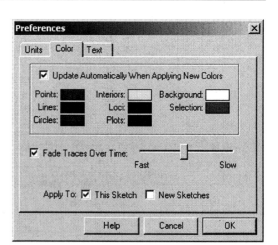

Update Automatically When Applying New Colors: When this box is checked, the preferences for your sketch are automatically changed whenever you color an object in the sketch. For example, if you color a line green and then construct a new segment, the new segment will also be colored green. Remove the check to have the preferences remain unchanged no matter how you modify the colors of objects in your sketch.

Even if Update Automatically When Applying New Colors is checked, you can prevent the preferences from being changed by holding down the Shift key while you change an object's color.

Object and Sketch Colors: The first six color rectangles show the default colors for various types of objects in Sketchpad: points, lines and other straight objects (segments, axes, and rays), circles and other curved objects (arcs), interiors, loci, and plots. New objects are assigned colors according to these settings. The last two color rectangles show the colors for selection markers and for the background of the sketch itself.

To change any of these colors, click the color rectangle you want to change. Your system's Color Picker dialog box appears, allowing you to choose a new color.

On a Macintosh, fading traces look best if your monitor display is set to Thousands or Millions of colors.

Fade Traces Over Time: Use this checkbox and speed control to determine whether or not traces fade and how fast they fade. When the box is checked, traces fade gradually over time, so recent traces are more vivid and older traces are fainter. If you remove this check, traces will never fade, and you'll have to remove them by using the **Erase Traces** command (or by pressing the Esc key). When fading is turned on, the speed control determines how quickly the traces fade.

See also: Trace (p. 148), Erase Traces (p. 149), Color (p. 8) Color Picker (p. 63)

Text Preferences

These settings control when objects are labeled, and whether or not the Text Palette appears automatically.

*Even if you don't show labels automatically, you can show (or hide) individual objects' labels by using the **Text** tool or **Show Labels**.*

```
============ Preferences ============
/ Units \ / Color \ / Text \

    Show Labels Automatically:
        □ For All New Points
        ☑ As Objects Are Measured

    ☑ Show Text Palette When Editing Captions

Apply To: ☑ This Sketch    [?] [Cancel] [ OK ]
          □ New Sketches
```

Show Labels Automatically: Check For All New Points to show the labels of new points when they're created. Check As Objects Are Measured to show labels when you measure an object. As you make a measurement, the labels needed to name the measurement will also appear. For example, if you measure the length of a segment between two unlabeled points, the segment endpoints' labels will also appear.

Show Text Palette When Editing Captions: If this box is checked, the Text Palette appears whenever you edit a caption and disappears when you finish editing. You can also display and hide the Text Palette by using the **Show Text Palette** command.

See also: Text Tool (p. 86), Show/Hide Labels (p. 147), Show/Hide Text Palette (p. 151), Text Palette (p. 53)

Advanced Preferences

This command allows you to change a variety of advanced settings that determine how Sketchpad works. Change these settings only after careful consideration; most users never need to modify them or need to modify them only once.

To use this command, hold down the Shift key before activating the Edit menu, causing the **Preferences** command to become **Advanced Preferences**.

Export Preferences

These settings control how sketches are printed and how Sketchpad objects are copied onto the clipboard.

Include Arrowheads: If this box is checked, printouts and pictures copied to the clipboard include arrowheads at the ends of lines, rays, and infinite point loci. If this box is not checked, the ends of these objects appear on printouts and on the clipboard just as they do in the sketch— with no special markings.

Locus/Plot Export Quality: The value displayed here determines how loci and function plots appear in printouts and on the clipboard. If the setting is 1x, such objects appear just as they do on the screen. Set the value to 5x to use five times as many samples or to 10x to use ten times as many samples. The default setting of 5x works well on most printers; you may want to change this to 10x for a very high-resolution printer. The higher the number of samples, the smoother the appearance of the curve.

Clipboard Image Scale: This value determines the magnification used for clipboard pictures. Set this to more magnification if you're copying pictures from Sketchpad to paste into a document in a word processor or page layout program that you intend to use for high-quality production. If you set the scale to more than 100%, the pasted picture will be large, and you'll have to scale it down in the word processing or page layout application into which you paste it. The result will be a higher-quality printout from the other application.

See also: Advanced Graphics Export (p. 223), Cut (p. 110), Copy (p. 110)

Sampling Preferences

These settings control the number of samples used for loci, function plots, and iterations. In general, the more samples, the more accurate or detailed the object appears, but the slower it is for Sketchpad to compute and draw. If your computer is faster than most, you may want to increase the values of these settings; if it's slow to draw and recalculate loci, plots, and iterations you may want to decrease these values.

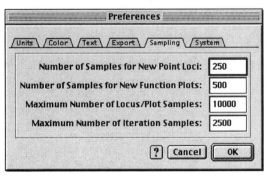

You can adjust the number of samples used in any specific locus or function plot by visiting its Plot Properties.

Number of Samples for New Point Loci: This value determines the number of samples used in a newly created point locus. (The number of samples in a new locus of a nonpoint object is proportionate to, but smaller than, this number.)

Number of Samples for New Function Plots: This value determines the number of samples used in a newly created function plot.

Maximum Number of Locus/Plot Samples: After you've created a locus or function plot, you can use **Properties** to change the number of samples. This value determines the largest number you can use in the Plot Properties panel when you're changing the number of samples for such an object.

Maximum Number of Iteration Samples: This value limits the number of samples allowed in an iterated image. For an iteration using a single map, this is the maximum number of iterations. For an iteration using more than one map, this value limits the depth in such a way that the total number of iterated images of a single object never exceeds this number.

See also: Loci (p. 24), Functions and Function Plots (p. 27), Locus (p. 163), Iterate (p. 178), Advanced Preferences (p. 138), Plot Properties (p. 124), Iteration Properties (p. 133)

System Preferences

These settings correlate Sketchpad's behavior with your particular computer, allow you to edit Sketchpad's color menu, and allow you to change all preferences back to their original values.

This value is "ideal" in the sense that Sketchpad attempts to reach it. If you're animating a particularly complex sketch or have a slower computer, animations may be slower than this.

Ideal Normal Speed: This value sets the approximate speed represented by a value of 1.0 in the Motion Controller, or "normal" speed for a Movement button. You should modify the speed only if your computer is consistently too fast or too slow for your tastes when animating objects at a speed of 1.0 in the Motion Controller.

Screen Resolution: This value sets the correspondence between the pixels on your computer screen and real-world length units. The normal value is 96 pixels/inch for Windows computers and 72 pixels/inch for Macintosh. You should modify this value only if it's absolutely necessary that on-screen distances match Sketchpad's measured distances. Changing this value may result in discrepancies when you paste Sketchpad pictures into other applications, which assume your screen resolution is fixed at 96 or 72 pixels/inch.

The Symbol font comes pre-installed on your computer.

Math Symbol Font: Sketchpad needs a symbol font so that it can display certain mathematical symbols such as π and θ. These symbols are normally found in the font called *Symbol*. If the Symbol font is not present on your computer, you can enter the name of a different font that contains the required symbols. If the Symbol font is missing or the alternative font you specify doesn't contain the needed symbols, Sketchpad won't be able to display those symbols correctly.

Edit Color Menu: This button displays your system's Color Picker dialog box, which allows you to change the colors in the Color menu. You can use this feature to add your favorite shades of magenta, teal, or chartreuse. If you create a sketch with a dark or black background, you may want to add white to the Color menu. (To edit the Color menu in Windows, see p. 142 for step-by-step instructions.)

Reset All Preferences: This button allows you to reset all Sketchpad preferences to their original values. Use it with care: you'll lose all the preferences values you've set in any other way.

See also: Motion Controller (p. 39), Animation Buttons (p. 36) Animate (p. 150), Animation Button (p. 112), Movement Button (p. 113), Color (p. 144), Color Picker (p. 63)

Editing the Color Menu in Windows

When you click the Edit Color Menu button on the Advanced Preferences System panel, the Edit Color Menu form of the Color Picker dialog box appears. Use this dialog box to set the colors that appear in Sketchpad's Color menu. The colors currently in the Color menu appear under Menu Colors.

1. Click one of the Menu Colors boxes to choose which menu color to change.

2. Use the HSL controls, the RGB controls, or the color box and slider on the right to set a new color.

3. Click Set New Color to change the menu color to your new color.

4. Click another of the Menu Colors to choose a different menu color to change.

5. Click OK when you're done, or Cancel to leave the Color menu unchanged.

See also: System Preferences (p. 140)

Display Menu

Display menu commands allow you to control the appearance of objects in your sketch and of the tools you use to work with them.

```
Display
   Line Width           ▶
   Color                ▶
   Text                 ▶
   Hide Objects      ⌘H
   Show All Hidden
   Show Labels       ⌘K
   Trace             ⌘T
   Erase Traces      ⌘B
   Animate           ⌘`
   Increase Speed    ⌘[
   Decrease Speed    ⌘]
   Stop Animation
   Show Text Palette ⇧⌘T
   Show Motion Controller
   Hide Toolbox
```

With these commands you can greatly enhance the visual appeal of a sketch and its effectiveness in communicating the mathematics it embodies. Using appropriate line widths and colors and hiding some objects while showing others help focus attention on the important parts of a sketch. Properly styled labels and captions help describe the purpose of the sketch and the mathematics behind it. Tracing and animation create dynamic visualizations of your sketch's underlying principles.

Line Width

These commands set the line width of each selected object to dashed, thin, or thick. Line width applies to straight objects, circles, arcs, loci, plots, and grids. To change an object's line width:

```
   Dashed      - - - - -
 ✓ Thin        ─────────
   Thick        ━━━━━━━
```

To change an object's line width without changing the setting for future objects, hold down the Shift key while choosing the command.

1. Select the object(s) whose line width you wish to change.

2. Choose the desired line width from the Line Width submenu of the Display menu.

When you change the selected object's line width, Sketchpad remembers your chosen width for future straight objects and curves in the current sketch.

When a grid is selected, the name of the command is **Dotted** rather than **Dashed**.

The Line Width setting has special effects on two types of objects—coordinate system grids and function and locus plots.

Line Width	Appearance of Grids	Appearance of Locus and Function Plots
Dotted (grids) or **Dashed** (plots)		
Thin		
Thick		

See also: Coordinate Systems (p. 21), Functions (p. 27), Loci (p. 24)

Color

These commands sets the color of each selected object.

To change an object's color without changing the setting for future objects, hold down the Shift key while choosing the command.

1. Select every object whose color you wish to change.

2. Choose the desired color from the Color submenu of the Display menu.

When you set the color of an object, Sketchpad remembers your chosen color for new objects of the same kind.

If you set the color of a caption that has different colors for different characters, choosing this command sets all of the characters to the new color you choose.

To change the color of an object's label, select the object and then choose the new color from the Text Palette.

If you set the color of a labeled geometric object, note that the color applies only to the object, not to its label.

You can change the color choices available in the Color submenu by using the System panel of the Advance Preferences dialog box.

See also: Color Preferences (p. 136), System Preferences (p. 140), Text Palette (p. 53)

Parametric Color

Parametric Color lets you "color by numbers." The number is provided by a Sketchpad value (such as a measurement). When the value changes, the color changes, too.

While you cannot color a locus or an iterated image parametrically, the locus or iterated image of a parametrically colored object will display the range of that object's colors.

Choose **Parametric** from the Color submenu to set the color of selected objects based on the numeric value of either one or three selected values.

This command is available only when you have selected one or three numeric values—measurements, calculations, or parameters—as well as one or more objects that can be colored parametrically—points, circles, arcs, straight objects, or interiors.

If you have selected one measurement, that

measurement is used to set a color from the spectrum (ranging from violet to deep red) or a grayscale color. You can set the Parametric Domain—that is, the numeric interval that corresponds to one complete cycle of the available colors or shades. You can also set the Color Range so that the cycle doesn't repeat, repeats one-way, or repeats bidirectionally.

If you have selected three measurements, all three measurements are used to determine the object's color. As with a single color, you can set the domain and color range. You can also decide whether the three measurements are interpreted as RGB (red, green, blue) values or as HSV (hue, saturation, value) settings.

Other Color

If your computer is set to display 256 or fewer colors, colors may not appear accurately, and you may be limited in your ability to select the color you want.

Choose **Other** from the Color submenu to set the color of the selected objects to a color other than those that appear in the Color submenu. Your system's Color Picker dialog box appears, allowing you to specify any color your computer can display.

See also: Color Picker (p. 63)

Text

The keyboard shortcut for **Increase Size** is Alt+> (Windows) or ⌘+> (Mac). The shortcut for **Decrease Size** is Alt+< (Windows) or ⌘+< (Mac).

This submenu sets the font used for the selected objects and can increase or decrease the font size for the selected objects.

Choose **Increase Size** to increase the font size for each selected object to the next-larger standard font size. Choose **Decrease Size** to reduce the font size for each selected object to the next-smaller standard font size.

If you want to set text styles such as bold, italic, or underline or if you want to set text size to a specific value, use the Text Palette.

See also: Text Palette (p. 53), Show Text Palette (p. 151)

Hide Objects

The keyboard shortcut for **Hide** is Ctrl+H (Windows) or ⌘+H (Mac).

This command hides each selected object from view, without changing its geometric role in the sketch. Use this command to hide objects that shouldn't be seen, but that are still required for geometric purposes in the sketch. When an object is hidden, it remains present in the sketch and can continue to define the position and behavior of other objects that remain visible.

If you have objects in your sketch that you don't want to see and that are *not* required for geometric reasons, it's better to delete those objects using the Backspace key or the **Clear** command than to hide them.

See also: Clear (p. 111), Show All Hidden (p. 146)

Show All Hidden

This command displays and selects all objects previously hidden in a sketch.

See also: Object Properties (p. 121), How to Show Just One Hidden Object (p. 147)

How To . . . Show Just One Hidden Object

In a sketch containing many hidden objects, you may want to show just one or two of those hidden objects. The **Show All Hidden** command shows all the hidden objects, and once you've shown them it can be a lot of trouble to reselect all of them in order to hide them again.

Here's a convenient way to show one particular object among many that have been hidden:

1. Choose **Show All Hidden** from the Display menu.

   All previously hidden objects appear and are selected.

2. Using a **Selection Arrow** tool, click on the object you wish to remain visible, deselecting it.

   The object you click is deselected; the other just-shown objects remain selected.

3. Choose **Hide** from the Display menu.

   The remaining selected objects are hidden, and the deselected object remains visible.

Another way to hide or show objects is by using the Hidden checkbox on the Object panel of the Properties dialog box. To display properties for a hidden object, you must first display properties for a parent or child of the hidden object, then choose the desired object from the Parents or Children pop-up menu.

See also: Object Properties (p. 121), Show All Hidden (p. 146), Hide Objects (p. 146), Object Relationships: Parents and Children (p. 10)

Show/Hide Labels

The keyboard shortcut for **Show/Hide Labels** is Ctrl+K (Windows) or ⌘+K (Mac).

This command shows or hides the label of each selected object. Most Sketchpad objects can show their labels, with a few exceptions such as grids, measurements and calculations, captions, pictures, and loci of objects other than points.

To show or hide labels:

1. Select every object whose label you wish to show or hide.

2. Choose **Show Labels** or **Hide Labels** from the Display menu.

Using this command is equivalent to clicking on an object with the **Text** tool.

When you measure a quantity that depends on a particular object, the object's label may automatically be shown if it's needed to display the measurement. For instance, if you measure the angle defined by three points, the labels of those points may be shown. Use the Text panel of **Preferences** to turn this automatic showing of labels on or off.

An object is labeled automatically when the label is first needed for some purpose—either because you've chosen the **Show Label** command, because you've clicked the **Text** tool on the object, or because you've measured some quantity that depends on the object. Thus the first point you label will become point *A,* even if it's the tenth point you've actually created in your sketch.

Although you can't show or hide the labels of measurements and calculations, you can control how they are named when they're displayed, using the Value panel of the Properties dialog box.

See also: Text Tool (p. 86), Text Preferences (p. 137), Label Properties (p. 121), Value Properties (p. 123)

Trace

The keyboard shortcut for **Trace** is Ctrl+T (Windows) or ⌘+T (Mac).

This command turns tracing on or off for each selected object. If all the selected objects are currently being traced, a check mark appears next to the command. Choosing the command turns tracing off for each selected object. If no check mark appears, choosing the command turns tracing on for each selected object.

When an object is traced, it leaves behind a trail as it moves, no matter how the motion is caused—whether by dragging the traced object, by dragging some object on which the traced object depends, or by animating.

Tracing can be useful for exploring how an object's movement is constrained or for creating interesting mathematical art.

The faster a traced object moves, the more spread out its trail; the slower the object moves, the denser its trail.

You can use Color Preferences to make traces gradually fade over time and eventually disappear. You can also control how fast traces fade—or turn off the fading of traces altogether. If fading is disabled, traces will remain on the screen indefinitely. To remove traces (whether fading or not) from the screen, choose **Erase Traces** from the Display menu.

Think of a trace as a temporary display of an object's locus. To construct a permanent locus, use the **Locus** command from the Construct menu.

There's an important difference between erasing traces and deactivating tracing for an object or objects. Erasing traces (using the **Erase Traces** command) removes all existing traces from the screen but has no effect on whether objects will leave traces in the future. Turning tracing off for an object (using the **Trace** command) prevents that object from leaving traces as it moves in the future, but has no effect on any traces the object has already left on the screen. If you want to remove all existing traces an object has left behind, and also to prevent that object from leaving traces in the future, you must use both commands:

1. Select the object and choose the **Trace** command to turn off future tracing for the object.

2. Choose **Erase Traces** to erase any existing traces from the screen.

See also: Erase Traces (p. 149), Color Preferences (p. 136), Loci (p. 24)

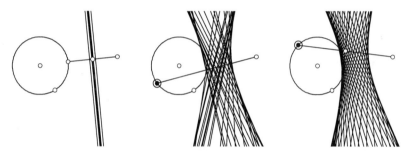

The perpendicular bisector of a segment attached to a circle is selected and traced (left). As the segment's endpoint is dragged around the circle, the bisector traces a hyperbolic envelope (center). Animating the endpoint around the circle results in smoother traces (right).

Erase Traces

The keyboard shortcut for **Erase Traces** is Ctrl+B (Windows) or ⌘+B (Mac).

This command removes all visible traces from the screen.

This command erases all traces immediately. If you want to control whether and how quickly traces fade, use the Color panel of the Preferences dialog box.

This command does not prevent traced objects from leaving new traces on the screen as they continue to move. To prevent an object from leaving new traces, you must select that object and turn tracing off for the object by choosing **Trace** from the Display menu.

You can also use the Esc key to erase traces.

See also: Trace (p. 148), Color Preferences (p. 136), Esc Key (p. 209)

Animate

The keyboard shortcut for **Animate** is Ctrl+` (Windows) or ⌘+` (Mac).

This command puts each selected geometric object into motion.

- Independent points move freely in the plane, in random directions.

- Points on paths move along their paths. Points on straight objects and arcs move bidirectionally. Points on circles and interiors move around their paths.

- Other objects move by moving the objects upon which they depend (that is, their parental objects).

This command has the same effect as pressing the Animate button on the Motion Controller.

Pause Animation and **Resume Animation** have the same effect as the Pause button on the Motion Controller.

When animations are running and nothing is selected, the **Animate** command becomes **Pause Animation**. When animation is paused, the command becomes **Resume Animation**.

You can also create Animation action buttons to start and stop specific animations.

See also: Stop Animation (p. 151), Increase Speed/Decrease Speed (p. 150), Motion Controller (p. 39), Animation Buttons (p. 36), Object Relationships: Parents and Children (p. 10)

Increase Speed/Decrease Speed

The keyboard shortcut for **Increase Speed** is Alt+] (Windows) or ⌘+] (Mac); for **Decrease Speed** it's Alt+[(Windows) or ⌘+[(Mac).

This command increases or decreases by about 25% the animation speed of each object that is both selected and animating, or of all animating objects if nothing is selected.

This command has the same effect as clicking on the speed control buttons of the Motion Controller.

If it's difficult to select the object whose speed you want to change, there are two methods you can use:

- Select any moving point by choosing from the Motion Controller's Target menu.

- Pause animation, select the desired object, and resume animation.

If nothing is selected, these commands change to **Increase All Speeds** and **Decrease All Speeds**.

See also: Animate (p. 150), Stop Animation (p. 151), Motion Controller (p. 39)

Stop Animation

If at least one selected object is moving, this command stops the motion of each selected moving object.

If nothing is selected but at least one object in the sketch is moving, this command changes to **Stop All Motions** and stops the motion of every moving object in the sketch.

This command has the same effect as pressing the Stop button on the Motion Controller.

You can also use the Esc key to stop all motion.

See also: Animate (p. 150), Motion Controller (p. 39), Esc Key (p. 209)

Show/Hide Text Palette

The keyboard shortcut for **Show/Hide Text Palette** is Shift+Ctrl+T (Windows) or Shift+⌘+T (Mac).

This command shows or hides the Text Palette. The Text Palette allows you to change the font, font size, and style for the label or text of each selected object.

If the palette is not currently showing, the command is **Show Text Palette**; if the palette is currently showing, the command is **Hide Text Palette**.

Use the Text panel of the Preferences dialog box to determine whether or not the Text Palette appears automatically when you create or edit a caption.

See also: Text Palette (p. 53), Text Preferences (p. 137)

Show/Hide Motion Controller

This command shows or hides the Motion
Controller.

Use the Motion Controller to control the
motion of the selected objects in your
sketch. The Motion Controller controls the
motion both of animated objects and of
objects set in motion by pressing a Movement button.

If the Motion Controller is not currently showing, the command is **Show
Motion Controller;** if it is currently showing, the command is **Hide Motion
Controller.**

The Motion Controller also appears automatically when you choose
Animate from the Display menu.

See also: Motion Controller (p. 39)

Show/Hide Toolbox

This command shows or hides Sketchpad's Toolbox.

If the Toolbox is not currently showing, the command is **Show Toolbox;**
if it is currently showing, the command is **Hide Toolbox.**

Hide the Toolbox to give you more space when you're working on a
large sketch or to remove the distraction of visible tools when you've
finished a sketch that should be manipulated only by using the **Selection
Arrow** tool to drag objects or to click on action buttons.

See also: Toolbox (p. 67)

Construct Menu

This menu provides commands for accomplishing many important geometric constructions. Most of these are constructions that could also be accomplished by using Sketchpad's **Compass** and **Straightedge** tools, but the Construct menu provides simpler and quicker ways of completing the construction.

Construct	
Point On Object	
Midpoint	Ctrl+M
Intersection	Ctrl+I
Segment	Ctrl+L
Ray	
Line	
Parallel Line	
Perpendicular Line	
Angle Bisector	
Circle By Center+Point	
Circle By Center+Radius	
Arc On Circle	
Arc Through 3 Points	
Interior	Ctrl+P
Locus	

Using the Construct Menu

Each command on the Construct menu requires you first to select one or more objects in the sketch. These selected objects are called the *selection prerequisites* of the construction: they are the objects to be used to define the construction itself. (For instance, to use the **Midpoint** command you must first select one or more segments.) Commands in the Construct menu are enabled only when you've selected appropriate prerequisites. If you want to use a command but find that it's disabled, check the objects you've selected in the sketch and compare them with the prerequisites listed in the description of that command.

If a command you wish to use is unavailable, it's possible you have *too few* or *too many* objects selected. Deselect unwanted objects or deselect all objects and try again.

See also: Compass Tool (p. 81), Straightedge Tools (p. 83)

Point On Object

Selection prerequisites: One or more path objects.

You can also construct a point on an object by clicking on it with the **Point** tool, or with any other tool that constructs points as part of its operation (such as the **Compass** tool, **Straightedge** tools, or most custom tools).

Constructs a point on each selected path object. The point is randomly placed on the object. It can later be animated or dragged anywhere on the object, but it will not leave the path.

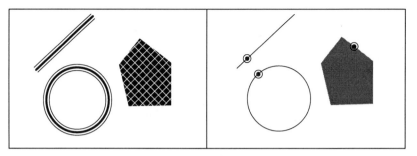

Path objects on which you can construct points include straight objects (segments, rays, and lines), curved objects (circles and arcs), interior objects (polygons and circle and arc interiors), point loci, and function plots. (When you use an interior as a path, the actual path is the perimeter of that interior. A point constructed on a polygon interior is free to move around the entire perimeter of the polygon.)

See also: Path Objects (p. 13), Objects (p. 8)

Midpoint

The keyboard shortcut for **Midpoint** is Ctrl+M (Windows) or ⌘+M (Mac).

Selection prerequisites: One or more segments.

Constructs a point at the midpoint of each selected segment. As a segment gets longer or shorter (through dragging an endpoint, for example), the midpoint moves accordingly.

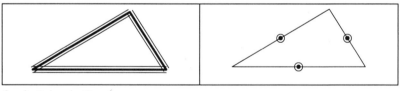

See also: Points (p. 9)

Intersection

The keyboard
shortcut for
Intersection is Ctrl+I
(Windows) or ⌘+I
(Mac).

*Selection prerequisites: Two intersecting objects, each of which is a straight object,
circle, or arc.*

Constructs a point at each intersection of the two selected objects. If
the objects actually intersect in two places, two points are constructed;
otherwise one point is constructed.

You can also
construct a point of
intersection by
clicking with the
Selection Arrow tool or
with any tool that
constructs points as
part of its operation
(such as the **Point**,
Compass, or
Straightedge tools).

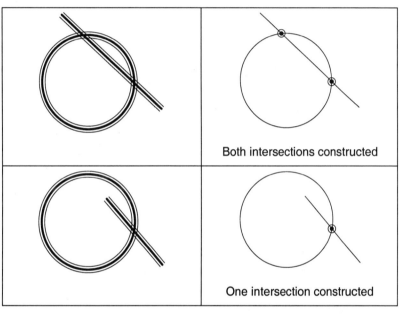

Both intersections constructed

One intersection constructed

If you later drag the intersecting objects apart, the constructed
intersection point disappears, and reappears when you drag the objects
so that they're again touching.

See also: Points (p. 9)

Segment, Ray, and Line

Selection prerequisites: Two or more points.

The keyboard
shortcut for **Segment**
is Ctrl+L (Windows)
or ⌘+L (Mac).

Constructs a segment, ray, or line through the selected points. (The **Ray**
command constructs a ray from the first point through the second.) If
more than two points are selected, this command constructs the same
number of segments, rays, or lines as the number of selected points.

(For instance, choosing **Line** with the four points *A*, *B*, *C*, and *D* selected will construct the four lines shown.)

To quickly construct a pentagon, hold down the Shift key while you click the **Point** tool five times. Then choose the **Segment** command to construct the five sides of the pentagon.

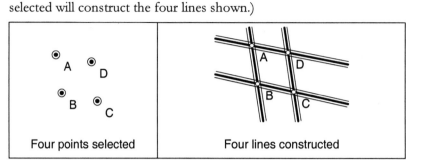

| Four points selected | Four lines constructed |

The results of these commands are the same as the results of using the **Straightedge** tools on the selected points. The commands are particularly useful for constructing multiple straight objects and for making sure that your straight objects go through the proper points.

See also: Straightedge Tools (p. 83), Segments, Rays, and Lines (p. 14)

Parallel Line

Selection prerequisites: A straight object and one or more points; or a point and one or more straight objects.

Constructs a line through each selected point parallel to each selected straight object.

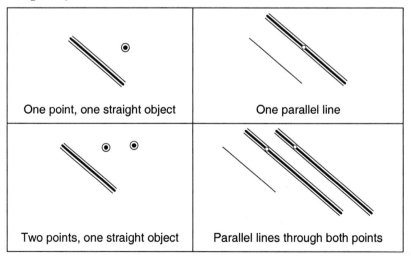

| One point, one straight object | One parallel line |
| Two points, one straight object | Parallel lines through both points |

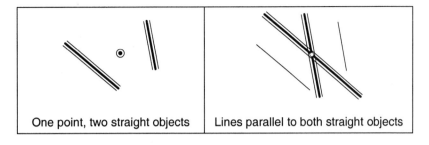

| One point, two straight objects | Lines parallel to both straight objects |

Perpendicular Line

Selection prerequisites: A straight object and one or more points; or a point and one or more straight objects.

Constructs a line through each selected point perpendicular to each selected straight object.

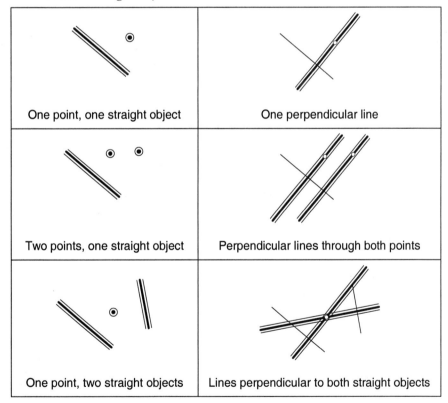

One point, one straight object	One perpendicular line
Two points, one straight object	Perpendicular lines through both points
One point, two straight objects	Lines perpendicular to both straight objects

Angle Bisector

Selection prerequisites: Three points, with the vertex point selected second.

Constructs a ray that bisects the minor angle formed by the three selected points. The second selected point designates the vertex of the angle. For instance, to bisect ∠*ABC*, select points in the order *A*, then *B*, and finally *C*.

See also: Segments, Rays, and Lines (p. 14)

Circle By Center+Point

Selection prerequisites: Two points.

Constructs a circle with its center at the first selected point and with its circumference passing through the second selected point. The result of this command is the same as the result of using the **Compass** tool on the two selected points.

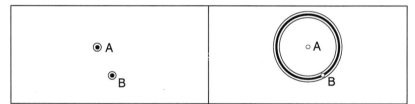

See also: Circles and Arcs (p. 15), Compass Tool (p. 81), Circle By Center+Radius (p. 159)

Circle By Center+Radius

Selection prerequisites: A point and one or more segments and/or distance measurements; or a segment or distance measurement and one or more points.

This command duplicates the function of a noncollapsible compass, which allows you to set a length, then draw circles centered anywhere with that length as the radius.

Constructs one or more circles centered at each selected point and with the radius determined by each selected segment or distance measurement.

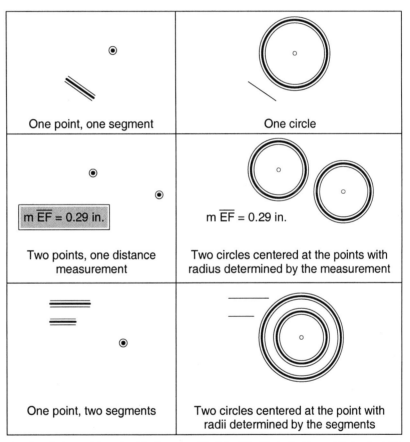

One point, one segment	One circle
m EF = 0.29 in. Two points, one distance measurement	m EF = 0.29 in. Two circles centered at the points with radius determined by the measurement
One point, two segments	Two circles centered at the point with radii determined by the segments

See also: Circles and Arcs (p. 15), Compass Tool (p. 81), Circle By Center+Point (p. 158)

Arc On Circle

Selection prerequisites: A circle and two points on that circle; or a center point and two other points equally distant from the center point.

The arc is constructed counter-clockwise from the first selected circumference point to the second. The order in which you select the points determines whether the constructed arc is a minor or major arc.

Constructs an arc on the given circle or with the given center, bounded by the selected circumference points.

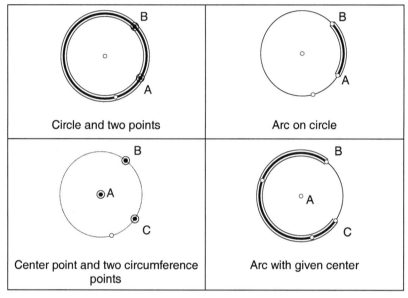

Circle and two points

Arc on circle

Center point and two circumference points

Arc with given center

Arc Through 3 Points

Selection prerequisites: Three noncollinear points; that is, three points that do not lie on the same line.

Constructs an arc through the three selected points. The arc starts at the first selected point, passes through the second, and ends at the third.

If subsequently you drag the three points collinear, the second point determines the arc's display. If the second point falls between the first and third, the arc has zero measure but nonzero arc length and displays as a straight segment from the first point through the second to the third. If the second point is collinear to, but outside of, the first and third, the arc disappears.

See also: Circles and Arcs (p. 15)

Interior

The keyboard shortcut for **Interior** is Ctrl+P (Windows) or ⌘+P (Mac).

Constructs the interior defined by the selected object or objects. Depending on your selection, one of four separate commands appears (**Polygon Interior, Circle Interior, Interior | Arc Sector,** and **Interior | Arc Segment**). A description of each follows.

Constructed interiors give your sketches substance and color and allow you to measure the areas and perimeters of figures. You can also use the perimeter or circumference of an interior as a path on which to construct or animate points.

See also: Polygons and Other Interiors (p. 16)

Polygon Interior

Selection prerequisites: Three or more points.

Constructs a polygon interior using the selected points as vertices. The order in which you select the points determines the order of the vertices of the polygon.

See also: Polygons and Other Interiors (p. 16)

Circle Interior

Selection prerequisites: One or more circles.

Constructs a circle interior for each selected circle.

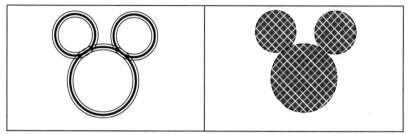

See also: Circles and Arcs (p. 15), Polygons and Other Interiors (p. 16)

Arc Sector Interior

Selection prerequisites: One or more arcs.

Constructs an arc sector interior for each selected arc. An arc sector is bounded by the arc and by the radii to the two endpoints of the arc.

See also: Arc Segment Interior (p. 162)

Arc Segment Interior

Selection prerequisites: One or more arcs.

Constructs an arc segment interior for each selected arc. An arc segment is bounded by the arc and by the chord connecting the two endpoints of the arc.

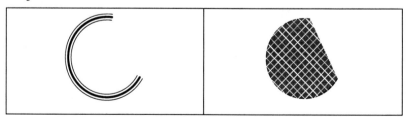

See also: Arc Sector Interior (p. 162)

Locus

Selection prerequisites: The object whose locus you want to construct (the driven object) and a point (the driver) that determines the position of that object. The driver must be constructed on a path; or you can select an independent point as the driver and a separate unrelated path object.

You can use Plot Properties to change the number of samples in a locus and to determine whether a point locus is displayed as discrete or continuous.

Constructs the locus of the selected object as the driver point moves along its path. Generally, a locus is the set of points (or other objects) that satisfies some mathematical condition. In Sketchpad, a locus is defined as the set of locations of an object—the *driven object*—whose position or shape is determined by the motion of a *driver* point as it moves along a path. You can construct loci of points, straight objects, circles, arcs, or interiors. The selected driver must be constructed as a **Point On Object** that controls the position of the driven object. Alternately, you may select as the driver an independent point that determines the position of the driven object, in which case you must also select an unrelated path along which the driver can travel.

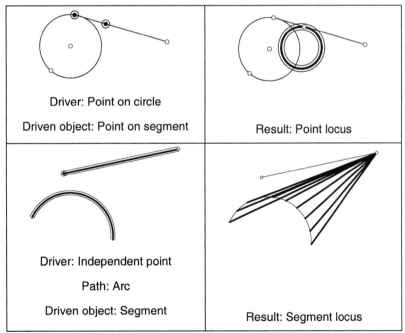

Driver: Point on circle	
Driven object: Point on segment	Result: Point locus
Driver: Independent point	
Path: Arc	
Driven object: Segment	Result: Segment locus

See also: Loci (p. 24), Path Objects (p. 13), Properties (p. 120), Point On Object (p. 153)

Transform Menu

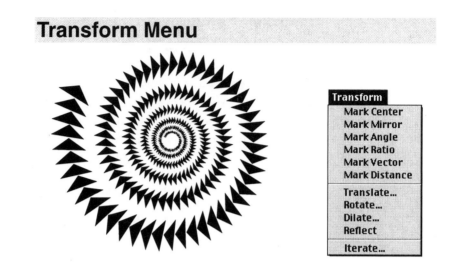

The Transform menu commands apply geometric transformations to figures in your sketches, allowing you to create translations, rotations, dilations, reflections, tessellations, scale models, kaleidoscopes, fractals, and much more. These commands include four basic transformations: **Translate** (to slide), **Rotate** (to turn), **Dilate** (to shrink or enlarge), and **Reflect** (to flip).

In addition to the object or objects that they transform—the transformational *pre-image*—each type of transformation involves certain *parameters:* objects or values upon which the transformation is based. For instance, a rotation requires both an angle and a center about which to rotate. The **Mark** commands—**Mark Center, Mark Mirror, Mark Angle, Mark Ratio, Mark Vector,** and **Mark Distance**—let you specify objects in your sketch to act as dynamic parameters for your transformations.

These parameters may be either geometric objects or geometric quantities. For example, a rotation is defined by two parameters: a center and an angle. The center is a geometric point about which objects rotate. The angle is a geometric quantity that determines how far objects rotate about the center.

The Transform menu provides a flexible set of commands that allow you to specify a rich variety of transformations using either fixed or dynamic transformational parameters. For instance, you can rotate a triangle by a fixed angle of 45° about some center point, or you might rotate by a dynamic parameter such as $\angle ABC$. (This is a "dynamic" parameter in the sense that if you then drag *A, B,* or *C,* the rotated image changes dynamically to the new ∠*ABC.*)

In general, follow these steps to construct the transformed image of one or more objects:

Once you mark a parameter, Sketchpad remembers that mark even after you change the selections. If you've already marked a parameter for one transformation, you don't need to mark it again to use the same parameter for a second transformation.

1. Mark any parameters that determine dynamic aspects of your transformation by selecting objects to define those parameters and choosing the appropriate **Mark** commands (for example, **Mark Center** to mark a selected point as the center of rotation).

2. Select the object(s) you wish to transform. (Mathematically, this is the *pre-image* of your transformation.)

3. Choose the appropriate transformation command from the Transform menu (for example, **Rotate**).

4. In the resulting dialog box, enter any fixed parameters you wish to use in your transformation (for example, type 45°) then leave the dialog box.

Sketchpad constructs the *image* of your selection according to the transformation and parameters you've specified.

Finally, the **Iterate** command allows you to create in a single step multiple transformed images such as the spiral shown above, or any figure resulting from a tranformation or construction repeated many times. Iteration can even be used to create complex images such as tessellations and fractals.

Mark Commands

Any marked object remains marked until you mark a new object of the same type. For example, you don't need to mark the same center more than once, no matter how many times you use it as a marked center.

The first six commands on the Transform menu allow you to mark the parameters to be used in subsequent transformations.

You can use most of the **Mark** commands whenever your selections include the required object(s) for that mark, even if you have other objects selected as well. Thus, if you've selected five polygons you want to dilate, then realize you forgot to mark the center, you can select your desired center point, without deselecting the polygons, and choose **Mark Center**. The most recently selected point is marked as the center and removed from your selections, and you can go ahead and choose **Dilate** for your polygons.

See also: Mark Center (p. 166), Mark Mirror (p. 166), Mark Angle (p. 166), Mark Ratio (p. 167), Mark Vector (p. 169), Mark Distance (p. 170)

Mark Center

If you haven't yet marked a center when you choose **Rotate** or **Dilate,** Sketchpad will automatically choose a point and mark it for you.

Marks the most recently selected point as the center point about which future rotations and dilations will take place. To mark a center:

- Select a point and choose **Mark Center** from the Transform menu, or

- Double-click a point with the **Selection Arrow** tool.

The marked point will flash briefly to indicate it's been marked as the center for future rotations and dilations. Once marked, this center point will be used for all future rotations and dilations until you mark a different center point.

You can also change the marked center while the Rotate or Dilate dialog box is open by clicking on the desired point in your sketch.

See also: Mark Commands (p. 165), Rotate (p. 174), Dilate (p. 176)

Mark Mirror

If you haven't yet marked a mirror when you choose **Reflect,** Sketchpad will automatically choose a straight object and mark it for you.

Marks the most recently selected straight object as the mirror across which future reflections will take place. To mark a mirror:

- Select a straight object and choose **Mark Mirror** from the Transform menu, or

- Double-click on a straight object with the **Selection Arrow** tool.

The marked straight object will flash briefly to indicate it has been marked as the mirror for future reflections. Once marked, this mirror will be used for all future reflections until you mark a different mirror.

See also: Mark Commands (p. 165), Reflect (p. 178)

Mark Angle

Use a marked angle for a transformation when you want your transformed image to move as the marked angle changes.

Marks the most recently selected angle or angle measurement as the angle to be used for future rotations and polar translations. To enable this command, your selections must include either three points or an angle measurement.

Rotations and polar translations can use either a fixed angle (such as 45°) or a marked angle (such as $\angle ABC$). When you rotate by 45°, the angle of rotation never changes, but when you rotate by $\angle ABC$, the rotation changes as the positions of points A, B, and C change.

You can mark an angle defined by three points, or you can mark an angle measurement or calculation.

Marking an Angle Using Three Points

1. Select the three points defining your angle. First, select a point on the initial side of the angle, then select the vertex, and finally, select a point on the terminal side of the angle.

For instance, if you select three points arranged as shown above, in the order *A, B, C,* the result will be a marked angle that specifies the counter-clockwise rotation shown by the arrow.

2. Choose **Mark Angle** from the Transform menu.

A brief animation from the initial side to the terminal side confirms that your angle has been marked.

Marking an Angle Measurement

1. Select the desired angle measurement, parameter, or calculation. The units of the value must be either degrees or radians.

2. Choose **Mark Angle** from the Transform menu.

The selection will flash briefly to confirm that your angle measurement, parameter, or calculation has been marked.

You can change the marked angle measurement while the Translate or Rotate dialog box is open by clicking on the desired measurement, parameter, or calculation in your sketch.

See also: Mark Commands (p. 165), By Polar Vector (p. 171), Rotate (p. 174), Angle (p. 189)

Mark Ratio/Mark Segment Ratio/Mark Scale Factor

Use a dynamic marked ratio or scale factor when you want your dilated image to change as the marked item changes.

Marks the most recently selected ratio or scale factor as the ratio for future dilations. This command displays one of three related appearances, depending on your selections. If you select:

- two segments, the command becomes **Mark Segment Ratio**. Dilation will use the ratio of the length of the first segment to the length of the second segment.

- a measured or calculated scale factor, the command becomes **Mark Scale Factor**. The selected measurement or calculation must be a scalar value (that is, a value without units).

- three collinear points, the command becomes **Mark Ratio**. If you select points A, B, and C in order, dilation will use the ratio of signed distances AC/AB.

Dilations can use either a fixed ratio (such as $\frac{1}{2}$) or a marked ratio (such as AC/AB). When you dilate by $\frac{1}{2}$, the ratio of dilation never changes, but when you dilate by AC/AB, the dilation changes as the positions of points A, B, and C change.

Marking a Ratio Using Two Segments

You can also mark a segment ratio *after* choosing **Dilate**. With the Dilate dialog box open, click on the first and then the second segment in your sketch.

1. Select a segment whose length will be used as the numerator of your ratio.

2. Select a second segment whose length will be used as the denominator.

3. Choose **Mark Segment Ratio** from the Transform menu.

You will see a brief animation confirming that the ratio has been marked.

If the first segment is shorter than the second, the ratio is less than 1 and dilation will shrink objects toward the marked center. If the first segment is longer than the second, the ratio is greater than 1 and dilation will stretch objects away from the marked center.

Marking a Scale Factor Using a Measurement, Parameter, or Calculation

You can also mark a scale factor *after* choosing **Dilate.** With the Dilate dialog box open, click on a measurement, parameter, or calculation that has no units.

1. Select a measurement, parameter, or calculation to be the scale factor. This value must be a pure number with no units (such as inches or degrees) associated with it.

2. Choose **Mark Scale Factor** from the Transform menu.

The selection will flash briefly to confirm that your measurement, parameter, or calculation has been marked.

If the magnitude of the value you marked as a scale factor is less than 1, the dilation will shrink objects toward the marked center. If the value's magnitude is greater than 1, the dilation will expand objects away from the marked center. If the scale factor is less than 0, image objects will be dilated "through the center," appearing on the opposite side of the center as their pre-images.

The Geometer's Sketchpad Reference Manual

Marking a Ratio Using Three Collinear Points

1. Select three collinear points in your sketch. The points must be in a straight line.

2. Choose **Mark Ratio** from the Transform menu.

You will see a brief animation confirming that the ratio has been marked.

When you mark three collinear points, A, B, and C, as a ratio, Sketchpad dilates by the ratio of signed distances AC/AB. If B is on the same side of A as C, the signed ratio of distances is positive; if B is on the opposite side of A as C, the ratio is negative. You may wish to use the **Ratio** command in the Measure menu to display this ratio numerically. One handy way to remember the role of the three selected points is to think of them as determining a ratio that, if the first selected point was the marked center, would dilate the second selected point to the location of the third selected point.

See also: Mark Commands (p. 165), Dilate (p. 176), Ratio (p. 192)

Mark Vector

You can also mark a vector using two points *after* choosing **Translate**. With the Translate dialog box open, click on the desired initial and terminal points in your sketch.

Marks for future translations the vector determined by the two most recently selected points. The first of these two points is the *initial* point of the vector, and the second is the *terminal* point of the vector.

When you choose this command, you will see a brief animation from the initial to the terminal point confirming that the vector has been marked.

After marking a vector, future translations for which you specify the By Marked Vector option will be based on this vector. Such translations will translate objects by a distance equal to the distance from the initial to the terminal point and in the same direction as the direction from the initial to the terminal point.

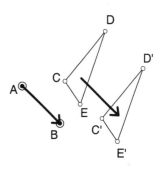

For instance, if you mark the vector from A to B as in the figure at right, then translate $\triangle CDE$, the result will be a second triangle translated by the distance from A to B and in the direction from A to B. As you adjust the vector by dragging *A* or *B,* the translated image of Δ*CDE* adjusts accordingly.

See also: Mark Commands (p. 165), Translate (p. 170)

Mark Distance

Marks the one or two most recently selected distance values (measurements, parameters, or calculations) to be used for future polar and rectangular translations.

You can also mark a distance *after* choosing **Translate.** With the Translate dialog box open, click on a distance measurement, parameter, or calculation in your sketch.

To mark a distance:

1. Select one or two distance measurements, parameters or calculations (ones with distance units, such as inches).

2. Choose **Mark Distance** from the Transform menu.

The selected distance value(s) will flash briefly to confirm that your distance has been marked.

If you choose **Mark Distance** with a single selected distance value, this new distance will become the marked distance for polar translation.

If you choose **Mark Distance** with two selected distance values, the first selected values will become the horizontal distance for rectangular translations, and the second will become the vertical distance.

See also: Mark Commands (p. 165), Translate (p. 170)

Translate

Sketchpad has both a **Translate Arrow** tool and a **Translate** command. When you use the tool, you translate the original object. When you use the command, you create a new object— a translated image of the original object.

Constructs a translated image of the selected geometric object(s).

To construct a translated image:

1. Select the geometric object(s) you wish to translate.

2. Choose **Translate** from the Transform menu.

    The Translate dialog box appears, and a translated image of your selections appears in the sketch.

3. Choose one of the Translation Vector options (Polar, Rectangular, or Marked), depending on how you wish to specify the translation. The Marked option is available only if you've already marked a vector; see Marked Translation Vector (p. 173) for more details.

The Geometer's Sketchpad Reference Manual

4. Specify any required values for the type of translation you've chosen. While you're choosing your values, you can see in the sketch a copy of the translated image that will be created.

5. You can click a distance measurement in the sketch to change the marked distance; you can click an angle measurement to change the marked angle; or you can click two points to change the marked vector.

6. When you're satisfied with the translation you've specified, click OK.

More detailed descriptions of the three Translation Vector options appear below.

See also: Dragging with the Translate Arrow Tool (p. 75), How to Construct a Segment of Fixed Length (p. 174)

Polar Translation Vector

When you specify a polar vector, a positive angle indicates counter-clockwise rotation, and a negative distance indicates clockwise rotation.

Choose this option to define the translation by specifying a distance and an angle.

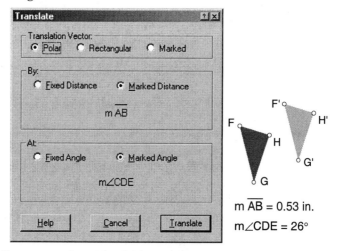

The distance can be a Fixed Distance (a number in your current distance unit), or it can be a Marked Distance (a distance measurement you've specified using the **Mark Distance** command). If you want to use a distance measurement that exists in your sketch but has not already been marked, you can click that measurement now to mark it.

The angle can be a Fixed Angle (a number in your current angle unit), or it can be a Marked Angle (an angle measurement you've specified using the **Mark Angle** command). If you want to use an angle measurement that exists in your sketch but has not already been marked, you can click that measurement now to mark it.

See also: Mark Distance (p. 170), Mark Angle (p. 166)

Rectangular Translation Vector

Choose this option to define the translation by specifying a horizontal distance and a vertical distance.

When you specify a rectangular vector, positive distances indicate translation to the right or up, and negative distances indicate translation to the left or down.

Each of these distances can be a Fixed Distance (a number in your current distance unit), or a Marked Distance (a distance measurement you've specified using the **Mark Distance** command). If you want to use a distance measurement that exists in your sketch but has not already been marked, you can click that measurement now to mark it. When you click a distance measurement in the sketch, the measurement you click becomes the marked vertical distance and the previous marked vertical distance becomes the marked horizontal distance.

See also: Mark Distance (p. 170)

Marked Translation Vector

Choose this option to define the translation by specifying a vector's initial and terminal points.

This option is enabled only if you've already marked a vector in your sketch. If you haven't already used the **Mark Vector** command to mark a vector, you can mark one now by clicking two points in your sketch—first the initial point, then the terminal point.

See also: Mark Vector (p. 169)

How To . . . Construct a Segment of Fixed Length

Note that these steps give you a fixed length and a fixed orientation. If you want a segment of fixed length whose orientation you can change, construct a circle with radius AA'. Then draw a second radius from A to any point B on the circle. Segment AB can now be dragged to any orientation while always having a fixed length, because all radii of the circle have the same length and the circle is constructed to always have a radius of fixed length AA'.

Occasionally you may wish to create a segment of fixed length—for instance, a segment that is exactly 1.5 cm in length. While you could create a segment with the **Segment** tool, measure its length, and drag one endpoint until its length was 1.5 cm, this segment would not be constructed to be fixed at 1.5 cm long. That is, dragging an endpoint again would change it from its current length to some other length.

To fix a segment's length in Sketchpad, you need to construct the segment in such a way that dragging cannot change its length. For an arbitrary length, the easiest way to do this is with the Transform menu.

1. Create a point A in your sketch.

2. Select point A and choose **Translate** from the Transform menu. In the dialog box, enter the fixed length as the distance by which you wish to translate point A.

3. Click on Translate.

Sketchpad constructs a new point A' as the translated image of A by the distance that you entered (1.5 cm). Now use the **Segment** tool to construct the segment between A and A'. No matter how you drag either endpoint, the segment's length will remain 1.5 cm because it has been constructed to always have that length.

Rotate

Sketchpad has both a **Rotate Arrow** tool and a **Rotate** command. When you use the tool, you rotate the original object. When you use the command, you create a new object—a rotated image of the original object.

Constructs a rotated image of the selected object(s). To rotate objects:

1. If you haven't already done so, select a point to act as the center for rotation and choose **Mark Center** from the Transform menu. Alternatively, you can double-click the desired center point with the **Selection Arrow** tool.

A brief animation indicates that the point has been marked as a center for subsequent rotations and dilations.

If you rotate without first marking a center, Sketchpad will mark one for you.

2. Select the object(s) you wish to rotate.

3. Choose **Rotate** from the Transform menu.

The Rotate dialog box appears, and a rotated image of your selections appears in the sketch.

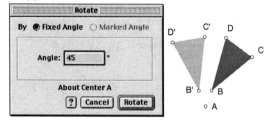

4. Choose either Fixed Angle or Marked Angle, as described below.

5. You can click a point in the sketch to change the marked center, or you can click an angle measurement to change the marked angle.

6. When you have chosen the options you want and entered any required values, click Rotate.

The rotated image appears.

Fixed Angle

Positive angles result in counter-clockwise rotations, and negative angles result in clockwise rotations.

Choose this option to enter a fixed (numeric) angle of rotation using your sketch's current angle units.

Marked Angle

Choose this option to rotate your selection based on an angle you've specified using the **Mark Angle** command. This choice is disabled if you haven't already marked an angle. However, if you want to use an angle measurement that exists in your sketch but has not already been marked, you can click that measurement now to mark it.

See also: Mark Center (p. 166), Mark Angle (p. 166), Dragging with the Rotate Arrow Tool (p. 75)

How To . . . Construct an Angle of Fixed Measure

Occasionally you may wish to create an angle of fixed measure—for example, an angle that measures exactly 33°. While you could create an angle by measuring three points and dragging them until they form an angle of 33°, this angle would not be constructed to be *fixed at* 33°. That is, dragging it again would change it from its current magnitude to some other magnitude.

To fix an angle in Sketchpad, you need to construct the angle in such a way that dragging cannot change its magnitude. For an arbitrary angle, the easiest way to do this is with the Transform menu.

1. Place two points, *A* and *B,* in your sketch.

2. Select point *A* and choose **Mark Center** from the Transform menu. Point *A* becomes marked as the center of future rotations and dilations.

3. Select point *B* and choose **Rotate**. In the dialog box, enter the fixed angle by which you wish to rotate.

4. Sketchpad constructs point *B'* as the rotated image of *B* by your requested angle. Even if you drag *A, B,* or *B',* Sketchpad will maintain this angle's magnitude, because you've defined *B'* to be the rotated image of *B* by this angle.

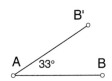

You can now construct rays or segments connecting *A, B,* and *B'* to incorporate the fixed angle into your sketch.

Dilate

Sketchpad has both a **Dilate Arrow** tool and a **Dilate** command. When you use the tool, you dilate the original object. When you use the command, you create a new object—a dilated image of the original object.

Constructs a dilated image of the selected object(s). In a dilated image, a particular ratio is used to move every point of the original closer to or farther away from the center point. If the ratio is greater than 1, the image points are farther away from the center than the originals and the image is larger than the original image. If the ratio is less than 1, the image points are nearer the center and the image is smaller.

To dilate objects:

1. If you haven't already done so, select a point to act as the center for dilation and choose **Mark Center** from the Transform menu. Alternatively, you can double-click the desired center point with the **Selection Arrow** tool.

   A brief animation indicates that the point has been marked as a center for subsequent rotations and dilations.

   If you dilate without first marking a center, Sketchpad will mark one for you.

2. Select the object(s) you wish to dilate.

3. Choose **Dilate** from the Transform menu.

   The Dilate dialog box appears, and a dilated image of your selection(s) appears in the sketch.

4. Choose either Fixed Ratio or Marked Ratio, as described below.

5. You can click a point in the sketch to change the marked center, you can click a measurement with no units to set the marked scale factor, or you can click two segments to set the marked segment ratio.

6. When you have chosen the options you want and entered any required values, click on Dilate.

The dilated image appears.

Fixed Ratio

A ratio smaller than 1 results in an image that's smaller than the original, and a ratio greater than 1 results in an image that's larger.

Choose this option to enter a fixed ratio by entering both numerator and denominator.

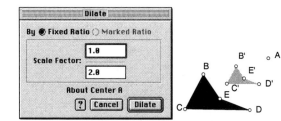

Marked Ratio

Choose this option to dilate your selection based on a marked ratio or scale factor you've specified using the **Mark Ratio** command. This choice is disabled if you haven't already marked a ratio. However, if you want to use a ratio of two segments that exist in your sketch, you can click the segments now to mark them. Similarly, if you want to use a measured scale factor that exists in your sketch, you can click it now to mark it.

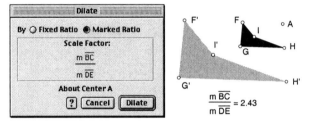

See also: Mark Center (p. 166), Mark Ratio (p. 167), Dragging with the Rotate Arrow Tool (p. 75)

Reflect

This command constructs a mirror image of the selected object(s) across a marked mirror. To reflect objects:

A shortcut for marking a straight object as a mirror is to double-click it.

1. Select a straight object (line, segment, ray, or axis) to be the mirror for reflection. Then choose **Mark Mirror** from the Transform menu. (If you don't already have a marked mirror and you skip this step, Sketchpad will mark a mirror for you.)

   A brief animation indicates that the straight object has been marked as a mirror for subsequent reflections.

2. Select the object(s) you wish to reflect.

3. Choose **Reflect** from the Transform menu.

The reflected image appears.

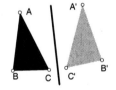

See also: Mark Mirror (p. 166)

Iterate

This command constructs the iterated images of a set of related geometric objects according to an iteration rule that you define. The command is available when you select some combination of pre-image points and pre-image calculations.

Pre-image points must be independent points or points on path, and must define other points (the image points) in your sketch. Pre-image calculations must be parameters or independent calculations, and must define both image calculations and geometric objects.

See the "Iterations and Iterated Images" topic in the Objects chapter (p. 31) for a more detailed description of iteration and related concepts such as iteration rules, pre-images, images, seeds, and orbits.

See also: Iterations and Iterated Images (p. 31)

Iterating by Example

In Sketchpad, you define an iteration rule by example, creating both pre-image and image and specifying how they correspond to each other.

For instance, the figure at right starts with *ΔABC*. *ΔDEF* is the midpoint triangle, constructed using as its vertices the midpoints of the sides of *ΔABC*.

To repeat this construction, you'd construct a new midpoint triangle using the midpoints of the sides of *ΔDEF*, and then another using the midpoints of the sides of that triangle, and so forth.

To specify this repetition as an iteration rule in Sketchpad, you define a map that identifies the image for each pre-image:

$$A \Rightarrow D$$

$$B \Rightarrow E$$

$$C \Rightarrow F$$

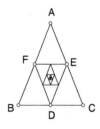

Even though the repeated construction includes the sides of the triangles as well as the vertices, you specify the rule using only points *A, B, C, D, E,* and *F*. Sketchpad figures out what other objects depend on the pre-image points and includes them in the iteration. In this example, Sketchpad will include the sides of the triangle in the iteration.

For best results, construct the entire pre-image but construct only the points of the image. Let Sketchpad construct the other parts of the image.

For example, to iterate the midpoint triangle, construct the pre-image (ΔABC) and the image points (midpoints D, E, and F), but not the remaining image objects (the segments connecting D, E, and F). Once you've constructed these objects, select the independent points that define the pre-image (points A, B, and C) and choose **Iterate** from the Transform menu.

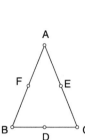

You may need to drag the dialog box out of the way so that you can see your original triangle and its midpoints.

Sketchpad displays the dialog box shown at right, allowing you to define the corresponding image for each selected pre-image point. For each pre-image point in the triangle, click on the midpoint to which that pre-image should map. As you click each midpoint, Sketchpad displays the results of iterating the pre-image triangle towards your mapped images. Once you've mapped each of the three pre-image points to a unique midpoint, click Iterate to confirm the iteration rule and close the dialog box.

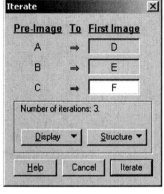

*You can use **Iterate** to create fractals by specifying more than one mapping of your pre-images to first images. See Multiple Iteration Maps (p. 182) for more information.*

Sketchpad produces a set of iterated images for each object affected by your mapping. In this example there are six iterated images, one for each vertex and side of your original triangle. You can select and manipulate each iterated image separately. For example, you could hide or delete the three iterated images of your original triangle's vertices, or you could color each of the three iterated images of your original triangle's edges with a different color. You can also use Iteration Properties to change the number of iterations that Sketchpad displays.

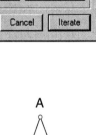
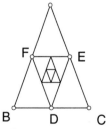

See also: Iterations and Iterated Images (p. 31), Iteration Properties (p. 133)

Using the Iterate Dialog Box

To construct the iterated images of one or more objects:

1. Select the initial pre-image objects whose positions or values define the iteration. You may select independent points, points constructed on paths, or independent parameters as your initial objects. (In other words, initial objects must be objects whose positions or values are not fully determined by other objects. Objects whose position or value depends on these initial objects will be iterated automatically as you iterate the initial objects.)

2. Choose **Iterate** from the Transform menu.

   The Iterate dialog box appears.

Drag the Iterate dialog box out of the way if it's hiding the destination images you want to click.

3. For each selected pre-image, click the corresponding first image of that object to which the pre-image maps during the iteration. For a pre-image point, click a dependent image point to which it should move during the iteration. For a pre-image parameter value, click a dependent calculated value. Images must be objects that are defined in terms of your pre-images, so that their position or value changes as the pre-image changes.

   As you specify each destination image, a partial iteration appears in the sketch corresponding to the matches you've specified so far.

4. You can use the Display pop-up menu to change the appearance of the iteration. See Display Options (p. 182) for a description of the available options.

5. You can use the Structure pop-up menu to change the structure of the iteration. See Structure Options (p. 182) for a description of the available choices.

6. Once you've specified the destination for each of the selected pre-images, click Iterate to finalize the iteration.

The constructed iteration appears. Use Iteration Properties to change the depth or other characteristics of the iteration.

See also: Iterations and Iterated Images (p. 31), Iteration Properties (p. 133)

Display Options

While you're using the Iterate dialog box, you can use the Display pop-up menu to control the appearance of the iteration. You can:

- increase or decrease the number of times your rule is iterated.

While there are exceptions, in general you may find it convenient to display all iterations when you're iterating a single map, and to display only the final iteration when you're iterating more than one map simultaneously. See Multiple Iteration Maps (p.182) for more information.

- display all iterations, or only the final iteration. The set of all iterated images of an object is sometimes called the *orbit* of that object.

Structure Options

While you're using the Iterate dialog box, you can use the Structure pop-up menu to control the structure of the iteration. You can:

- add a new iteration map or remove the current map (see Multiple Iteration Maps, p. 182).

- create images of all objects that depend on the selections or create images of only the nonpoint objects. (Often—especially when working with multiple maps—you won't want to see the iterated images of points, but only of segments, polygons, and so forth. Sketchpad automatically switches this option for you—to only create nonpoint object images—when you start working with multiple maps, though you can switch it back if you prefer to create point images as well as nonpoint images.)

- set iterated points on objects to stay at the same relative location as the original or set them to use new random locations each time they're iterated. (See Random Iterated Points, p. 183.)

Multiple Iteration Maps

By specifying a destination point for each of the iterated independent points, you create a single iteration *map*. This map describes how to transform the pre-image to create a transformed copy of the original objects. For most iterations, each iteration step produces a single copy of the original objects. For such iterations, the iteration rule consists of a single map.

The Geometer's Sketchpad Reference Manual

But for other iterations, one step of the iteration produces two or more copies of the original objects. Each such copy of the original objects requires its own map, so such iterations require multiple maps. For example, a parallelogram tessellation requires you to iterate the original parallelogram both horizontally and vertically.

Fractals and tessellations are the most common geometric constructions for which the iteration rule requires multiple iteration maps.

To construct an iteration with multiple maps, specify the first map as in steps 1–3 above. Then choose **Add New Map** from the Structure pop-up menu and specify a second map by clicking in turn on a new destination for each of the original points. When you're finished specifying all the maps that make up your iteration rule, click Iterate.

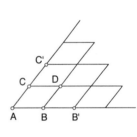

How To . . . Construct a Sierpinski Gasket

Because iteration can be applied to *any* type of Sketchpad construction, the options that support it may at first seem bewilderingly complex. The best way to develop an understanding of iteration is to work through examples. In this example, you'll use iteration to define a fractal known as the Sierpinski gasket. This fractal is the limit of the process of replacing a triangle by three smaller interior triangles; then replacing each of these three interior triangles by three even smaller triangles; and so on. Since at each stage you are replacing a pre-image triangle by three different image triangles, you'll need three mappings to define the fractal.

1. In a new sketch, use the **Segment** tool to construct a $\triangle ABC$ in your sketch.

2. Construct the midpoints of your triangle's edges. Use the Text tool to label the vertices *A, B,* and *C,* and the midpoints *D, E,* and *F,* as in the illustration below.

You now have a pre-image triangle and—implicitly—many smaller triangles, such as ΔAFE, ΔEBD, and so forth. Note that the three smaller triangles, ΔAFE, ΔFBD, and ΔEDC, form the interior "corners" of your original triangle.

3. Select the three points *A, B,* and *C,* and choose **Iterate** from the Transform menu.

Note that in this step you map *B* to itself, as this vertex is the same in both the original triangle and in the lower-left corner triangle.

4. In the Iterate dialog box, map $A \Rightarrow F$, $B \Rightarrow B$, and $C \Rightarrow D$. This maps the original triangle to the lower-left corner Δ *FBD*. You should see a series of triangles iterating into the lower-left corner of your original triangle.

5. Use the Structure pop-up menu to add a new mapping to your iteration rule. In the new mapping, map $A \Rightarrow E$, $B \Rightarrow D$, and $C \Rightarrow C$. This now iterates your pre-image triangle to the lower-right, while simultaneously—by the previous map—iterating each image to the lower-left.

6. Use the Structure pop-up menu again to add a third and final mapping to your iteration rule. In this third mapping, map $A \Rightarrow A$, $B \Rightarrow F$, and $C \Rightarrow E$. This iterates your previous mappings toward the upper corner of the triangle.

7. Click the Iterate button to dismiss the dialog.

With your completed iteration selected, you can increase or decrease the number of displayed iterations by pressing the + or – key on the keyboard.

Be careful not to increase the number of iterations too quickly. Since each iteration adds three times as many new triangles as the previous iteration, the construction quickly becomes very complex! Sketchpad will start to slow down if your sketch contains iterations more complex than your computer can handle gracefully.

If you could iterate an infinite number of times, the result of this process would be a Sierpinski gasket. If you imagine the area of your initial triangle as having been replaced by the area of three smaller triangles at each step, think for a moment about what happens to the total area of all of the smaller triangles as you increase the number of iterations. Since the three smaller triangles didn't cover the initial triangle, the area must be getting smaller. Thus with each iteration the area becomes smaller. What's the limit of the area? How do you know? What happens to the perimeter? Fractals frequently give rise to surprising properties.

You can visualize the areas by repeating the above steps in a new sketch, using a $\triangle ABC$ in which you have used **Polygon Interior** to construct the triangle interior. When you're done specifying your three mappings and have dismissed the Iterate dialog box, be sure to select and hide the original interior of $\triangle ABC$ so you can see the iterated smaller triangle interiors "inside" your original triangle interior.

Random Iterated Points

After you've constructed an iteration, you can use its Iteration Properties to experiment with both choices for how to iterate points constructed on path objects.

Sometimes you may find yourself specifying a point on an object as the first image of an iterated pre-image. For instance, rather than map a triangle's vertices to its midpoints as in the previous example, you might map a triangle's vertices to arbitrary points constructed on its three segment edges. In this case, the Structure pop-up menu gives you the choice of how you want Sketchpad to iterate these arbitrary points on objects. When you choose **To Same Relative Location,** Sketchpad displays each iterated image point at the same relative location as that first image you chose in the Iterate dialog box. If you drag that first image point to a new position on the path on which it's constructed, all of the iterated images adjust to the same relative new position. On the other hand, if you choose **To New Random Locations,** each iterated image of your initial point appears at a new, random location on its (iterated) path, independent of the location of the first image. This choice is useful if you're exploring geometric probability or other applications of randomness.

-- Move Points On Objects --
✔ To Same Relative Location
To New Random Locations

See also: Point On Object (p. 153), Iteration Properties (p. 133)

Parametric Depth

If an iteration's depth is determined by the value of a parameter or calculation, you can't use Properties to change the depth.

When you define an iteration, you can use a measurement, parameter, or calculation in your sketch to determine the depth of the iteration. After you select the points or parameters that define the pre-image, but before you choose the **Iterate** command, also select the value to be used in defining the iteration depth. Hold down the Shift key while you pull down the Transform menu, and the **Iterate** command becomes **Iterate To**

Depth. Choose this command and use the Iterate dialog box to define the iteration normally. Once the iteration is defined, the integer part of the value of the selected measurement, parameter, or calculation is used to determine the iteration depth. (If the value is negative, the depth is set to zero. If the value is too large to display all the iterated images, Sketchpad uses the maximum depth at which the images can be displayed.)

Terminal Point

You cannot construct a terminal point on an iteration that uses multiple iteration maps.

On occasion you may want to make use of the very last point of an iterated point object. You may want to attach a construction to this point, or you may want to measure some quantity that depends on the point.

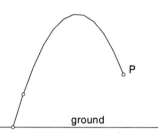

Distance P to ground = 1.75 cm

When you select an iterated point image, the **Iterate** command changes to **Terminal Point**.

To construct the terminal point of an iterated point image, select the iterated image of the point. From the Transform menu, choose **Terminal Point**. The terminal point of the iterated point image is constructed. If the depth of the iteration changes, the terminal point moves accordingly.

In the example above, an iteration was used to construct the flight path of a thrown ball. (The pre-image points, not shown here, defined the initial velocity of the ball and the strength of gravity.) To determine the height of the ball after some number of iterations, the terminal point was constructed and used to measure the distance between the terminal point and the ground.

Measure Menu

The Measure menu commands allow you to measure numeric properties of selected objects. The commands in the top portion of the menu measure objects' geometric properties; the commands in the bottom portion measure analytic properties. The Measure menu also contains a powerful calculator that allows you to derive new properties by calculating relationships between existing measurements. For example, you can use **Calculate** to sum the measured interior angles of a triangle or compute the ratio of a circle's measured circumference to its radius.

Measure	
Length	
Distance	
Perimeter	
Circumference	
Angle	
Area	
Arc Angle	
Arc Length	
Radius	
Ratio	
Calculate	Alt+=
Coordinates	
Abscissa (x)	
Ordinate (y)	
Coordinate Distance	
Slope	
Equation	

If you want to measure a specific property and its command is not available, make sure you have only that command's prerequisites selected. (You may have too many or too few objects selected.)

To measure an object's properties, select that object and choose from the available commands in the Measure menu. Sketchpad produces a measurement—a named numeric value in the proper units—as the result. When you drag or change an object that you've measured, the measured value changes accordingly.

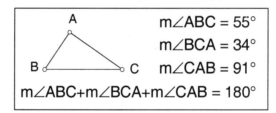

$$m\angle ABC = 55°$$
$$m\angle BCA = 34°$$
$$m\angle CAB = 91°$$
$$m\angle ABC + m\angle BCA + m\angle CAB = 180°$$

Three measurements and a calculation

Each command in the Measure menu is available only when objects appropriate to that measurement are selected. In other words, like those in the Construct menu, commands in the Measure menu require certain *selection prerequisites*.

Here's a summary of the selection prerequisites for each command:

To use this command:	Select:
Length	one or more segments
Distance	two points, or one point and one straight object
Perimeter	one or more polygon, arc sector, or arc segment interiors
Circumference	one or more circles or circle interiors
Angle	three points (select the vertex second)
Area	one or more interiors or circles
Arc Angle	one or more arcs, or a circle and two or three points on the circle
Arc Length	one or more arcs, or a circle and two or three points on the circle
Radius	one or more circles, circle interiors, arcs, or arc interiors
Ratio	two segments or three collinear points
Calculate	(always enabled)
Coordinates	one or more points
Abscissa (x)	one or more points
Ordinate (y)	one or more points
Coordinate Distance	two points
Slope	one or more straight objects
Equation	one or more lines or circles

See also: Measurements, Calculations, and Parameters (p. 18), Selection Arrow Tools (p. 70)

Length

The length of a segment is equal to the distance between its endpoints.

Selection prerequisites: One or more segments.

Measures the length of each selected segment, using the distance units chosen on the Units panel of the Preferences dialog box.

See also: Units Preferences (p. 135)

Distance

Selection prerequisites: Two points, or one point and one straight object.

To measure the distance between two points on a coordinate system in grid units, use the **Coordinate Distance** measurement instead.

Measures the distance between two points, or the distance from a point to a straight object, using the distance units chosen on the Units panel of the Preferences dialog box.

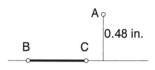

Distance A to $\overline{BC}$ = 0.48 in.

The distance from a point to a line is the shortest distance from the point to the line and is measured along the perpendicular. The distance from a point to a ray or segment is defined to be the same as the distance from the point to the straight line that contains the ray or segment.

See also: Units Preferences (p. 135), Coordinate Distance (p. 195)

Perimeter

Selection prerequisites: One or more polygon, arc sector, or arc segment interiors.

Measures the perimeter of each selected polygon or arc interior, using the distance units chosen on the Units panel of the Preferences dialog box. The perimeter of an arc sector is the sum of the arc length and the lengths of the two radii bounding the arc sector. The perimeter of an arc segment is the sum of the arc length and the length of the chord bounding the arc segment.

See also: Units Preferences (p. 135), Coordinate Distance (p. 195)

Circumference

Selection prerequisites: One or more circles or circle interiors.

Measures the circumference of each selected circle or circle interior, using the distance units chosen on the Units panel of the Preferences dialog box.

See also: Units Preferences (p. 135)

Angle

Selection prerequisites: Three points.

When measuring an angle, always select the vertex second.

Measures the angle defined by the three selected points, using the angle units chosen on the Units panel of the Preferences dialog box. The first selected point defines the initial side of the angle, the second defines the vertex, and the third defines the terminal side of the angle.

If angle units in Preferences are set to **directed degrees** or **radians**, the value of the measurement can be either positive or negative. A counter-clockwise angle results in a positive measurement, and a clockwise angle results in a negative measurement. Possible values range from –180° to +180°, or from –π radians to π radians.

If the angle units are set to **degrees**, all angle measurements are positive, between 0° and 180°.

See also: Units Preferences (p. 135), Arc Angle (p. 191)

Area

Selection prerequisites: One or more interiors or circles.

Measures the area of each selected polygon interior, circle, circle interior, arc segment interior, and arc sector interior, using the distance units chosen on the Units panel of the Preferences dialog box.

See also: Units Preferences (p. 135)

Arc Angle

Arc Angle (sometimes also called *arc measure*) refers to the *central* angle—that is, the angle formed by the radii connecting the circle's center to the endpoints of the arc, as shown at right.

Selection prerequisites: One or more arcs, or a circle and two or three points on the circle.

If one or more arcs are selected, this command measures the angle of each selected arc, using the angle units chosen on the Units panel of the Preferences dialog box. If the angle units in Preferences are set to **degrees** or **directed degrees**, the value ranges from 0° to 360°. If the angle units are set to **radians**, possible values range from 0 radians to 2π radians.

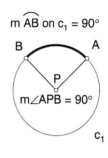

If a circle and two points are selected, this command measures the angle of the minor arc on the circle defined by the two selected endpoints. If the angle units in Preferences are set to **degrees**, possible values range from 0° to 180°. If the angle units in Preferences are set to **directed degrees**, values range from −180° to 180°; clockwise arcs result in negative values, and counter-clockwise arcs result in positive values. If the angle units are set to **radians**, possible values range from $-\pi$ radians to π radians.

If a circle and three points are selected, this command measures the angle of the minor or major arc that starts at the first selected point, passes through the second, and ends at the third. If the angle units in Preferences are set to **degrees**, possible values range from 0° to 360°. If the angle units in Preferences are set to **directed degrees**, possible values range from −360° to 360°; clockwise arcs result in negative values, and counter-clockwise arcs result in positive values. If the angle units are set to **radians**, possible values range from -2π radians to 2π radians.

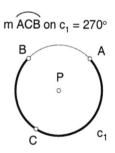

See also: Units Preferences (p. 135), Angle (p. 190)

Arc Length

Selection prerequisites: One or more arcs, or a circle and two or three points on the circle.

If one or more arcs are selected, this command measures the length of each selected arc, using the distance units chosen on the Units panel of the Preferences dialog box. If a circle and two points are selected, this command measures the length of the minor arc on the circle defined by the two selected endpoints. If a circle and three points are selected, this command measures the length of the minor or major arc on the circle that starts at the first selected point, passes through the second, and ends at the third.

See also: Units Preferences (p. 135)

Radius

Selection prerequisites: One or more circles, circle interiors, arcs, or arc interiors.

The radius of an arc is the same as the radius of the circle on which the arc falls.

Measures the radius of each selected circle, circle interior, arc, arc sector interior, or arc segment interior, using the distance units chosen on the Units panel of the Preferences dialog box.

See also: Units Preferences (p. 135)

Ratio

Collinear points are points that lie on the same straight line.

Selection prerequisites: Two segments or three collinear points.

If two segments are selected, this command measures the ratio of the lengths of the segments. The length of the first selected segment is the numerator of the ratio, and the length of the second is the denominator.

If three collinear points A, B, and C are selected, this command measures the ratio of the distance from A to C divided by the distance from A to B. If points B and C are on the same side of A, the ratio is positive; if B and C are on opposite sides of A, the ratio is negative.

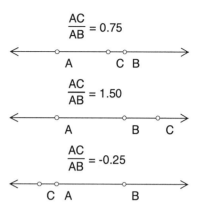

Another way to think of the ratio defined by three collinear points is to think of a number line with its origin at point A and its unit point at B. The position of point C on this number line determines the value of the measurement.

How To . . . Construct a Slider

You can also create a numeric value directly, using the **New Parameter** command from the Graph menu. The advantage of the slider described here is that sliding the control point back and forth provides a powerful, visual way to change the value.

Often it is useful to construct a *slider* for controlling a numeric value. For example, if you wanted to create a graph of the line $y = mx + b$ in which you can slide a point back and forth to control the values of m and b, you might want to set up sliders for m and b. To make a slider for m:

1. Construct a line through two points A and B.
2. Use the **Point** tool to construct a point C on the line.
3. Select A, B, and C in that order, and choose **Ratio** from the Measure menu.

$$\frac{AC}{AB} = 0.61$$

←———○———————○———○—→
　　　　A　　　　　C　　B

4. Select and hide the line and point B, leaving only two points and the measured ratio.
5. Construct a segment from A to C.

$$\frac{AC}{AB} = 0.61$$

○—————————○
A　　　　　　C

6. Double-click the measured ratio with the **Text** tool, and set its label to *m*.

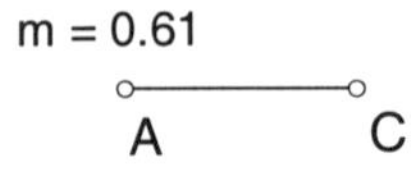

m = 0.61

A   C

Your basic slider is complete. As you drag *C,* the value of *m* changes accordingly. If you want, you can improve on the slider by hiding *A,* by hiding the label of *C* or changing *C*'s label to something more meaningful, or by using **Calculate** to multiply *m* by a constant, creating a new value that spans a larger (or smaller) range than the original value of *m* as you drag *C*.

Calculate

Selection prerequisites: None.

This command displays the
Calculator and allows you   m∠ABC+m∠BCA+m∠CAB = 180.00°
to create a calculation in
the sketch. The calculation can use constants and mathematical operations, and it can use measurements, calculations, and parameters that already exist in the sketch. The calculation can also use Sketchpad's standard functions as well as any user-defined functions that already exist in the sketch.

See also: Calculator (p. 47), New Function (p. 202), Calculations (p. 18)

Coordinates

Selection prerequisites: One or more points.

Measures the coordinates of each selected point with respect to the marked coordinate system. If there is no marked coordinate system, Sketchpad marks an existing coordinate system or creates a new one.

If the coordinate system is square or rectangular, the coordinates are measured in (x, y) form. If the coordinate system is polar, the coordinates are measured in (r, θ) form.

See also: Abscissa (p. 195), Ordinate (p. 195), Grid Form (p. 199), Coordinate Systems and Axes (p. 21)

Abscissa (x)

Selection prerequisites: One or more points.

Measures the abscissa (x value) of each selected point with respect to the marked coordinate system. If there is no marked coordinate system, Sketchpad marks an existing coordinate system or creates a new one.

See also: Coordinates (p. 194), Ordinate (p. 195), Grid Form (p. 199), Coordinate Systems and Axes (p. 21)

Ordinate (y)

Selection prerequisites: One or more points.

Measures the ordinate (y value) of each selected point with respect to the marked coordinate system. If there is no marked coordinate system, Sketchpad marks an existing coordinate system or creates a new one.

See also: Coordinates (p. 194), Abscissa (p. 195), Grid Form (p. 199), Coordinate Systems and Axes (p. 21)

Coordinate Distance

Selection prerequisites: Two points.

Measures the distance between the two points based on the marked coordinate system. If there is no marked coordinate system, Sketchpad marks an existing coordinate system or creates a new one.

This command differs from the **Distance** command because the coordinate distance is based, not on physical distance (that is, not on inches or centimeters), but on the unit size of the marked coordinate system. A coordinate distance measurement has no units.

See also: Distance (p. 189), Coordinates (p. 194), Coordinate Systems and Axes (p. 21)

Slope

Selection prerequisites: One or more straight objects.

Measures the slope of each selected line with respect to the marked coordinate system. If there is no marked coordinate system, Sketchpad marks an existing coordinate system or creates a new one.

See also: Coordinate Systems and Axes (p. 21)

Equation

Selection prerequisites: One or more lines or circles.

Measures the equation of each selected object with respect to the marked coordinate system. If there is no marked coordinate system, Sketchpad marks an existing coordinate system or creates a new one.

The equation of a line is expressed in one of the following three forms:

- $y = c$ for a vertical line

- $x = c$ for a horizontal line

- $y = m \cdot x + b$ for any other line

For a circle, the equation is expressed in one of the following two forms:

In other words, a Euclidean circle described by an equation in square coordinates has a circle's equation. The same shape, described in nonsquare coordinates, has the equation of an ellipse.

- $(x-h)^2 + (y-k)^2 = r^2$ if the coordinate system is square

- $\dfrac{(x-h)^2}{a^2} + \dfrac{(y-k)^2}{b^2} = 1$ if the coordinate system is nonsquare

See also: Coordinate Systems and Axes (p. 21), Grid Form (p. 199)

The Geometer's Sketchpad Reference Manual

Graph Menu

The Graph menu allows you to create and manipulate coordinate systems, to create parameters and functions, to find the derivative of a function, and to plot points and functions on the coordinate axes. The coordinate axes and the coordinate system that the axes define form the foundation for investigations and activities in analytic geometry and algebra.

Graph	
Define Coordinate System	
Mark Coordinate System	
Grid Form	
Show Grid	
Snap Points	
Plot Points...	
New Parameter...	
New Function...	Ctrl+F
Plot New Function...	Ctrl+G
Derivative	

In addition to the commands on the Graph menu, the commands at the bottom of the Measure menu allow you to measure various quantities on the coordinate plane, including coordinates of points, coordinate distances between points, slopes of straight objects, and equations of lines and circles.

See also: Coordinates (p. 194), Abscissa (p. 195), Ordinate (p. 195), Coordinate Distance (p. 194), Slope (p. 196), Equation (p. 196)

Define Coordinate System

If you choose a command, such as **Measure | Coordinates,** that requires a coordinate system but you haven't created one in your sketch, Sketchpad defines and marks a coordinate system for you.

This command creates a new coordinate system and marks it as the active coordinate system. The type and scale of the created coordinate system depends on your selections, as described in this table.

Selections	Command	Result
One point	**Define Origin**	Square coordinate system centered on the selected point with default unit scale
One circle	**Define Unit Circle**	Square coordinate system centered on the selected circle with unit scale determined by the circle's radius
One defining distance*	**Define Unit Distance**	Square coordinate system centered on a default origin with unit scaling determined by the defining distance

One point and one defining distance*	**Define Unit Distance**	Square coordinate system centered on the selected point with unit scaling determined by the defining distance
Two defining distances*	**Define Unit Distances**	Rectangular coordinate system centered on a default origin, with horizontal unit scaling determined by the first selected distance and vertical unit scaling determined by the second selected distance
One point and two defining distances*	**Define Unit Distances**	Rectangular coordinate system centered on the selected point with horizontal unit scaling determined by the first selected distance and vertical unit scaling determined by the second selected distance
Nothing or anything other than the above	**Define Coordinate System** (disabled if there's already a marked coordinate system)	Square coordinate system with default origin and unit scaling

* A *defining distance* can be either a segment or a distance measurement or calculation.

As described in the table, some commands define a coordinate system with a default origin or default unit scaling. Sketchpad constructs a default origin as an independent point in the center of your window. The default unit scale is equal to the current distance unit chosen in the Preferences dialog box, but can be adjusted by dragging the coordinate system's unit point or axis tick labels.

Since most activities require only a single coordinate system, the last command choice (which defines an entirely default coordinate system) is disabled if your sketch already has a coordinate system. If you really want a second coordinate system, you must select the appropriate objects as listed in the first column of the table.

See also: Coordinate Systems and Axes (p. 21), Mark Coordinate System (p. 199)

Mark Coordinate System

Selection prerequisites: a coordinate system's axis, origin point, unit point, unit circle, or grid

This command marks the coordinate system associated with the selected object as the coordinate system on which to measure or plot new objects.

When you have multiple coordinate systems, one of those coordinate systems is the *marked* coordinate system. All of the Graph menu commands apply to the marked coordinate system, as do those Measure menu commands that require a coordinate system.

The marked coordinate system is normally the most recently created coordinate system; you use this command to mark a different coordinate system.

Normally you'll have only a single coordinate system, and you won't have to worry about which coordinate system is marked.

See also: Define Coordinate System (p. 197), Coordinate Systems and Axes (p. 21)

Grid Form

Use this command to change the grid appearance and scaling of the marked coordinate system.

Sketchpad's coordinate systems can have three possible forms:

If the horizontal and vertical axes of a polar coordinate system have different scaling, the constant-distance grid lines appear as ellipses rather than circles.

- **Polar Grid:** A polar coordinate system has a set of grid lines that are circles (constant distance from the origin, or *r* value) and a set of grid lines that pass through the origin (constant angle from the origin, or θ value). Any coordinate system can be made polar.

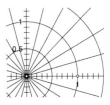

- **Square Grid:** A square coordinate system has the same scaling on the horizontal and vertical axes and has horizontal (constant *y* value) and vertical (constant *x* value) grid lines. Any

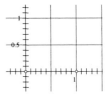

coordinate system except one defined in terms of two different distances can be made square.

- **Rectangular Grid:** A rectangular coordinate system has independent scaling for the horizontal and vertical axes and has horizontal (constant y value) and vertical (constant x value) grid lines. Any coordinate system except one defined in terms of a unit circle can be made rectangular.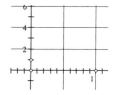

If you choose one of these commands with a sketch that doesn't yet have a coordinate system, Sketchpad creates a default coordinate system with the chosen form.

See also: Show Grid (p. 200)

Show Grid

This command shows or hides the grid lines of the marked coordinate system.

When the grid of the marked coordinate system is showing, the command changes to **Hide Grid**.

If you choose **Show Grid** with a sketch that doesn't yet have a coordinate system, Sketchpad creates a default coordinate system.

If you press the Shift key when you activate the Graph menu, the command changes to **Show Coordinate System** or **Hide Coordinate System**, and has the effect of showing or hiding the grid, the axes, and the origin of the marked coordinate system.

See also: Grid Form (p. 199), Snap Points (p. 200)

Snap Points

Use **Snap Points** when you want to work with "nice" whole-number coordinates.

When active, this command causes independent points to snap to nearby locations when you create or drag them. Choose this command once to activate it. When snapping is active, a check-mark appears next to the command. Choose the command a second time to deactivate snapping.

The locations to which points snap when this command is active depend on the grid form of the marked coordinate system. For square and rectangular grids, points snap to locations with whole number

The Geometer's Sketchpad Reference Manual

coordinates (that is, to the *integer lattice*). For polar grids, points snap to locations whose distance from the origin is a whole number and whose angle with respect to the horizontal axis is a multiple of 15°. In either case, points you create or drag when **Snap Points** is active only snap to locations that are relatively close by. In other words, if you have rescaled your coordinate system so that the distance between integer coordinates is great, points you create or drag will only snap to integer locations that are close to them.

See also: Grid Form (p. 199)

Plot Points/Plot As (x, y)/Plot As (r, theta)

This command plots one or more points on the marked coordinate system at the specified coordinate location. If there is no marked coordinate system, Sketchpad creates a default coordinate system.

If you have two selected measurements or calculations and there's a marked polar coordinate system, the command appears as **Plot As (x, y)** or **Plot As (r, theta)**. When you choose the command, Sketchpad creates a new plotted point at the coordinates determined by the two selected measurements, with the first measurement used as the *x* or *r* coordinate and the second as the *y* or *θ* coordinate. As the measurements change, the position of the plotted point changes to match.

If you don't have two selected measurements or calculations, the command is **Plot Points**. This command brings up a dialog box that allows you to plot one or more points on the marked coordinate system by entering the coordinates of each point to plot.

In the dialog box:

You can type numbers with decimal points, or you can type expressions such as 2+3 and π/4.

- Choose Rectangular to plot points using (*x, y*) values or choose Polar to plot them using (*r, θ*) values.

- Click Plot to plot the current values; the dialog box remains open to allow you to plot additional points.

- After plotting your last point, click Done to close the dialog box.

New Parameter

Use this command to create a new parameter in your sketch. A parameter is a number that can easily be changed. It's convenient to use parameters in places where you need to have a number but want to be able to change that number easily.

You can use parameters in calculations, in functions, and as values by which to transform objects. For example, you might create two parameters, named m and b, and use them in plotting the function $y = mx + b$. Or you might create a parameter that varies from 0° to 360° and use it as a marked angle to rotate a polygon.

When you choose **New Parameter**, a dialog box appears.

> **Name:** You can type a new name for the parameter. If you want the name to have a subscript, enter the subscript within square brackets at the end of the name. For example, the default name t[1] appears as t_1 in the sketch.

> **Value:** You can set the initial value of the parameter by typing a value in this field.

> **Units:** You can choose whether the parameter's value uses no units, uses the current angle unit, or uses the current distance unit.

See also: Measurements, Calculations, and Parameters (p. 18), Units Preferences (p. 135), Animate (p. 150), Edit Parameter (p.119)

To change the value of a parameter, you can double-click it with the **Arrow** tool, use the **Animate** or **Edit Parameter** commands, or create an Animation action button.

New Function

This command displays the Calculator and allows you to create a new function in the sketch. The function can use constants and mathematical operations, and it can use measurements, calculations, and parameters that already exist in the sketch. The function can also use Sketchpad's standard functions as well as other user-defined functions that already exist in the sketch.

$$f(x) = a \cdot x^2 + b \cdot x + c$$

See also: Calculator (p. 47), Functions (p. 27), Plot Function (p. 203)

Plot Function/Plot New Function

Use this command to plot one or more selected functions or to create and plot a new function if no objects are selected.

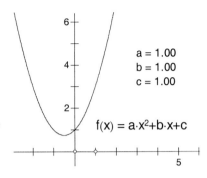

a = 1.00
b = 1.00
c = 1.00

$f(x) = a \cdot x^2 + b \cdot x + c$

If you're plotting a new function, the Calculator appears, just as it does for the **New Function** command, to allow you to define the function to be plotted.

Once you've plotted a function, you can change the domain or the number of samples by using the Plot Properties dialog box. You can also change the domain by dragging the arrows at the ends of the function plot.

To change the form of the function plot—to plot your function f as a polar function $r = f(\theta)$ or as an inverse plot $x = f(y)$—change the equation of the function itself. (To do this, select the function and choose **Edit Function** from the Edit menu. When the Calculator appears, choose the form you want from the Equation pop-up menu.)

See also: Calculator (p. 47), Properties (p. 120), Editing Functions (p. 29), Functions and Function Plots (p. 27), Plot Properties (p. 124), New Function (p. 202)

Derivative

This command creates a new function that is the derivative of the selected function with respect to that function's independent variable.

$f(x) = x \cdot \sin(x)$
$f'(x) = x \cdot \cos(x) + \sin(x)$

- Derivative functions update automatically when the function they differentiate is edited.

- In most ways derivative functions behave just like other functions you create. You can calculate with derivative functions, evaluate derivative functions for specific arguments, and plot derivative functions. You can even create the derivative of a derivative. The only thing you can't do with derivative functions is to edit them directly; you must edit the original function instead.

- Differentiation of complicated functions can be time-consuming. In these cases, a dialog box like the one at right appears. Click Cancel if you wish to interrupt computation of an exact derivative. If you cancel, Sketchpad will provide you with an approximate derivative, in the form

$$f'(x) = \frac{f(x+0.005) - f(x-0.005)}{0.01}$$

See the chapter on Sketchpad's Internal Mathematics (p. 234) for a more detailed discussion of derivatives.

This approximate derivative can still be plotted, and can even be differentiated itself. Although there is some loss in accuracy, in most cases the approximation resembles the exact derivative.

See also: Functions and Function Plots (p. 27)

Window Menu

This menu is available only for The Geometer's Sketchpad for Windows.

This menu includes commands for arranging your open document windows on the screen and for navigating among those documents.

Window
Cascade
Tile
1 Poincare disk.gsp - Segment
2 Shapes.gsp
3 Sliders.gsp
✔ 4 Congruence.gsp - SSA

Cascade

Arranges all open document windows in an overlapping fashion, starting from the top left of the main Sketchpad window.

Tile

Arranges all open document windows as tiles within the main Sketchpad window.

Window List

Choose a document from this list to bring that document's window in front of all other document windows. This list contains up to ten documents, with a checkmark indicating the document whose window is in front of all other document windows.

More Windows...

This command appears at the bottom of the window list when you have more than ten open document windows. Use this command to bring to the front a window that doesn't appear among the first ten in the list.

Help Menu

The Help menu contains commands that you can use to get help on using Sketchpad. The Sketchpad help system is an electronic version of this *Reference Manual,* including information on all of Sketchpad's commands and tools, contains a myriad of useful tips and techniques, and provides a table of contents and index to make it easy for you to find the information you're looking for.

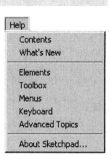

Windows users can press F1 while pointing to a menu command to get help on that command, even if the command is disabled. Windows users can also press F1 when a dialog box is open to get help on that dialog box.

Contents takes you to the first page of the help system, from which you can get an overview of Sketchpad's help system, access the various help topics, and look up specific terms and phrases.

What's New gives you a summary of the differences between Sketchpad Version 3 and Sketchpad Version 4, and also provides information about any new features or late-breaking news which is not in the printed documentation.

Elements describes the windows, pages, and tools of Sketchpad documents; the various kinds of objects you can create; and the Motion Controller, Text Palette, and Calculator.

Toolbox provides information on using the tools in Sketchpad's toolbox.

Sketchpad's help system is only available on computers that have a web browser installed.

Menus allows you to quickly find information about using any of Sketchpad's menu commands.

Keyboard describes the various keyboard shortcuts available in Sketchpad, and the special features you can take advantage of by using the keyboard.

Advanced Topics describes several advanced features of Sketchpad that are of particular interest to experienced Sketchpad users.

About Sketchpad appears here in the Windows version only; it appears on the Apple menu in the Macintosh version. This command displays a dialog box identifying the registered user name, the specific version number of the program, and assorted program information and credits.

In addition to the Help menu, most of Sketchpad's dialog boxes have Help buttons that you can click to get specific information about using that dialog box.

Context Menu

The Context menu provides a convenient shortcut to many of the menu commands that apply to a specific document or object. The Context menu does not appear in the main menu itself; it appears only when you request it.

To display the Context menu:

Windows: Click the right mouse button in your sketch.

Mac: Hold down the Ctrl key while you click in your sketch.

When the Context menu appears, if there's room on the screen, the menu appears in such a position that either **Preferences** or **Properties** is directly under the mouse. This makes it especially easy to choose these commands.

The commands available in the Context menu depend on where in the sketch you click. If you click in empty space the Context menu contains commands that apply to your sketch as a whole. If you click on an object in your sketch, the Context menu contains commands that apply to that object. The Context menu always shows only available commands.

For information on any of the commands in the Context menu, refer to that specific topic in the Menu Reference.

See also: Menu Reference (p. 101)

| Close |
| Document Options... |
| Print... |
| Paste |
| Select All |
| Preferences... |
| Show Text Palette |
| Show Motion Controller |
| Hide Toolbox |
| Calculate... |
| Polar Grid |
| Square Grid |
| Rectangular Grid |
| Show Grid |
| Plot Points... |
| New Parameter... |
| New Function... |
| Plot New Function... |

Keyboard Reference

The keyboard provides a convenient way to access many of Sketchpad's functions, providing shortcuts to common menu commands as well as performing other operations. This section describes all of Sketchpad's keyboard actions.

Keyboard Menu Command Shortcuts

Many menu commands have shortcut keys, allowing you to access the menu command directly from the keyboard whenever that command is available. Most of these shortcuts require a modifier key (such as Alt or Ctrl on Windows or ⌘ on Mac) to be held down while you type the command's shortcut key. Shortcut keys (and their modifiers) are listed in the menu, directly across from the name of each command that can be accessed by a keyboard shortcut.

For example, in the Windows File menu the **Save** command lists Ctrl+S as its keyboard shortcut. In the Macintosh File menu it lists ⌘+S as its keyboard shortcut. Thus, you can save the active document by typing the S key while holding down the Ctrl modifier key (in Windows) or the ⌘ modifier key (on Macintosh).

See also: Menu Reference (p. 101)

The Esc Key

The Esc key provides a powerful general-purpose means to "escape from" your current activity. Depending on the activity you're presently engaged in, Sketchpad's response to the Esc key varies, but in general, Esc reverts Sketchpad to a less "special" state. Each press of the Esc key performs one of the following actions:

- If a caption is being edited, Esc stops editing the caption.

- If the **Arrow** tool is not active, Esc activates the **Arrow** tool.

- If any object is selected, Esc deselects all objects.

- If any object is animating, Esc stops all animations.

- If any traces are visible, Esc erases all traces.

Press Esc repeatedly to revert your document to a "normal" state, with no objects animating, no traces visible, no objects selected, and the **Arrow** tool active.

See also: Editing Captions (p. 88), Selection Arrow Tools (p. 70), Selecting and Deselecting Objects (p. 70), Stop Animation (p. 151), Erase Traces (p. 149)

Other Special Keys

Other keys perform special operations that affect your document's view and selected objects, or your choice of active tool in the Toolbox.

Key	Action
Delete *or* **Backspace**	Deletes selected object(s) (same as **Clear**).
↑, ↓, ←, *or* →	Drags the selected object(s) one pixel in the indicated direction. (Press and hold keys to drag longer distances.)
+ *or* **–**	When one or more loci or function plots are selected, increases (+) or decreases (–) the number of samples in those objects by a fixed percentage.
+ *or* **–**	When one or more iterated images are selected, increases (+) or decreases (–) the number of iterations by one.
+ *or* **–**	When one or more parameters are selected, increases (+) or decreases (–) those parameters' values. (Press and hold keys to continue adjusting values; use Parameter Properties to choose the keyboard adjustment factor for each parameter.)
Shift+↑ *or* **Shift+↓**	Changes the active tool to the next higher (Shift+↑) or lower (Shift+↓) tool in the Toolbox.
Shift+← *or* **Shift+→**	When the active tool is a **Selection Arrow** tool or a **Straightedge** tool, changes the active tool to the next or previous **Selection Arrow** or **Straightedge** in the Toolbox.
Alt (Windows) *or* **Option (Macintosh)**	Temporarily invokes drag-scrolling. Click and drag in your document to scroll it in an arbitrary direction. Release the Alt (Windows) or Option (Macintosh) key to resume the active tool.

Shift	Optional menu commands: Changes **Undo** to **Undo All**. Changes **Redo** to **Redo All**. Changes **Preferences** to **Advanced Preferences**. Changes **Iterate** to **Iterate To Depth**. Changes **Show/Hide Grid** to **Show/Hide Coordinate System**.
Shift-drag	Maintains a picture's aspect ratio while resizing.
Shift	Constrains straightedge tools.
Shift	When changing object or text appearance, preserves default settings for • Line Width • Color • Font • Style • Size
p (Windows) **Option+p (Macintosh**	Types π as part of a numeric value in a dialog box.

See also: Clear (p. 111), Dragging Objects (p. 73), Loci (p. 24), Functions and Function Plots (p. 27), Plot Properties (p. 124), Parameters (p. 19), Parameter Properties (p. 125), Iterations and Iterated Images (p. 31), Iteration Properties (p. 133), Toolbox Overview (p. 69), Undo (p. 109), Redo (p. 110), Advanced Preferences (p. 138), Parametric Depth (p. 185), Show Grid (p. 200), Pictures (p. 37), Constructing Straight Objects (p. 14)

Advanced Topics

Once you become familiar with the basic ideas behind Sketchpad—the organization of its tools and menus, and the process of creating and exploring mathematical ideas through Dynamic Geometry constructions—you may wish to explore some of the program's advanced options. This section contains expert tips for using Sketchpad efficiently; instructions for using Sketchpad to create both interactive Dynamic Geometry web pages for posting on the Internet and high-quality mathematical illustrations for use in other programs or in printed documents; and an overview of the program's internal mathematics.

Tips for Experts

As you gain experience in Sketchpad, you'll naturally seek ways to maximize your efficiency and productivity within the software environment. This chapter contains a miscellaneous assortment of recommendations and advanced techniques for using Sketchpad productively.

About Sketchpad's Menu Structure

Sketchpad's menus are arranged thematically. While the File, Edit, and Display menus contain commands relating to your Sketchpad documents and workflow, the other menus and tools are more mathematical in nature. Each of these menus presents a distinct mathematical viewpoint and commands appropriate to that viewpoint. Familiarizing yourself with their organizational structure can help you plan your approach to a given construction problem or mathematical challenge.

In that the **Compass** tool does not retain a fixed radius, it technically provides a collapsible, rather than a noncollapsible, compass.

- The Toolbox's **Compass** and **Straightedge** tools provide the fundamental tools of compass-and-straightedge Euclidean geometry.

- The Construct menu contains additional commands for working in compass-and-straightedge Euclidean geometry. (Many of the objects you create with this menu could be created with the **Compass** and **Straightedge** tools alone, though some would take many steps to create with those tools.) Where the **Circle By Center+Point** command is equivalent to the **Compass** tool, **Circle By Center+Radius** allows you to construct circles of a given radius, acting as a noncollapsible, rather than a collapsible, compass.

Since compass-and-straightedge geometry does not include tools for specifying lengths metrically, you cannot construct a segment of a given length—say, 5.0 cm—using only the Construct menu. However, since the Transform menu's operations *are* metric in nature, you can use its commands to produce such a result.

- The Transform menu contains commands drawn from the perspective of a metric transformational geometry. Use them to construct or explore symmetries and other transformational relationships. You may specify transformational parameters—such as angles of rotation or scaling factors of dilation—either geometrically, by referring to existing objects, or metrically, by entering numeric angles and lengths (or by referring to numerical values and calculations already defined in your sketch).

- The Measure menu's commands continue the metric theme and offer a variety of ways to determine numeric relationships in your construction. The commands that appear in this menu above the **Calculate** command can be thought of as ruler-and-protractor operations: They measure distances, areas, and angles using the metric units you choose in **Preferences**. The commands that appear after the **Calculate** command are analytic in nature and measure quantities in relationship to some (existing or newly-defined) coordinate system.

- Finally, the Graph menu's commands continue the analytic perspective and pursue it into algebra and calculus, offering operations relating to coordinate systems and to variables and functions considered abstractly.

While each of these menus reflects a unique mathematical perspective, in the course of any Sketchpad activity you may move back and forth between perspectives to focus on different aspects of your activity. In particular, move from a geometric or spatial visualization to a numeric perspective using commands from the Measure menu. (Think of these commands as "turning shapes into numbers.") Move from numbers back into geometric or spatial visualizations ("turn numbers into shapes") by using the **Plot as (x, y)** and **Plot Function** commands, or use Transform menu commands with marked numeric values as transformational parameters.

Finally, in addition to the commands that produce or construct specific mathematical relationships in your sketch, each menu contains one command that produces a *generalization* of an arbitrary set of such relationships over some change.

- The Construct menu's **Locus** command lets you visualize the *position* of a constructed object over a change in one point's position.

- The Transform menu's **Iterate** command lets you visualize the *orbit* of one or more objects over some number of repetitions of a construction.

- The Measure menu's **Calculate** command lets you express a general relationship arithmetically between two or more measured quantities.

- The Graph menu's **Plot Function** command lets you visualize a general function evaluated over a changing domain.

- The Toolbox's **Custom** tool lets you generalize a set of relationships constructed between objects into a new tool that you can use to replicate that construction on a new set of objects.

Mastering these advanced commands allows you to move beyond the specific mathematical relationships, objects, tools, and commands that form Sketchpad's starting points and opens up a set of mathematical curves, shapes, and construction tools limited only by your imagination.

See also: Menu Reference (p. 101), Locus (p. 163), Iterate (p. 178), Calculate (p. 194), Plot Function (p. 203), Plot as (x, y) (p. 201), Custom Tools (p. 90)

Selection Techniques

The **Select Parents** and **Select Children** keyboard shortcuts can be very useful when used together. For instance, if you have one side of a triangle selected, you can quickly select all three sides as follows:

1. Select the two adjacent vertices using the keyboard shortcut for **Select Parents**: Ctrl+U (Windows) or ⌘+U (Mac).

2. Select all three sides using the keyboard shortcut for **Select Children**: Ctrl+D (Windows) or ⌘+D (Mac).

Thus with one side selected you can quickly select all three sides by holding down the Ctrl or ⌘ key and pressing the keys U and then D. Similarly, with one side selected you can quickly select all three vertices by holding down the Ctrl or ⌘ key and pressing the keys U, D, and U.

The selection rectangle also provides a way of selecting several objects at once, and makes possible some useful shortcuts. Shown below are two common cases in which using a selection rectangle is significantly easier than clicking on the objects individually.

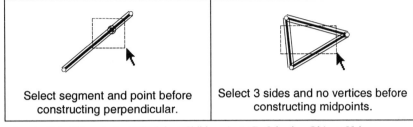

| Select segment and point before constructing perpendicular. | Select 3 sides and no vertices before constructing midpoints. |

See also: Select Parents (p. 115), Select Children (p. 115), Selecting Objects Using a Selection Rectangle (p. 71), Object Relationships: Parents and Children (p. 10)

Using Shortcuts

Using Sketchpad's shortcuts can significantly reduce the amount of time you spend navigating the menus and manipulating tools in the Toolbox. Menu command keyboard shortcuts are listed in the menus next to the commands themselves, but be sure to review the Keyboard Reference section for a list of keyboard shortcuts beyond those that correspond to menu commands.

Two shortcuts are worth special mention to the expert.

- The Esc key is a general-purpose shortcut for "escaping from" any special program activity and returning the program to a more basic state. Use the Esc key to deselect all objects and to revert to the **Arrow** tool without using the mouse. If you are animating or displaying the traces of animated objects, Esc can stop your animations and erase their traces as well. Repeatedly pressing Esc causes Sketchpad eventually to revert to its most basic state, with no objects animating or selected, no traces visible, and the **Arrow** tool active in the Toolbox.

To display an element's Context menu when clicking on that element, click with the right mouse-button in Windows, or click while holding down the Ctrl key on a Macintosh.

- The Context menu is a general-purpose shortcut for displaying only the menu commands that are available and appropriate to a clicked-on program element. Use the Context menu to display commands appropriate to a single sketch object by clicking on that object or to a single document by clicking in blank space within that document's window. When you click on a sketch object, Sketchpad displays the Context menu for that object with **Properties** as the default command choice. When you click in a document's blank space, Sketchpad displays the Context menu for that document with **Preferences** as the default command choice. These default choices make the Context menu the most convenient way to access these two powerful dialog boxes, each of which allows you to modify the appearance and behavior of your chosen object or document.

See also: Keyboard Reference (p. 209), Context Menu (p. 207), Properties (p. 120), Preferences (p. 134)

Expressions in Dialog Boxes

To enter π in a dialog box, type p (in Windows) or Option+p (on a Macintosh).

Many of Sketchpad's dialog boxes permit or require you to enter various numeric quantities. Wherever you're required to enter a number, you can substitute an arithmetical expression—such as (1/3) or 2π—instead. Type expressions combining numbers, parentheses, addition (+), subtraction (–), multiplication (*), division (/), and exponentiation (^). Sketchpad evaluates your expression and uses the resulting value for the dialog box quantity.

Command-Line Flags for Sketchpad (Windows Version)

With the Windows version of Sketchpad you can set several command-line flags that determine Sketchpad's start-up behavior. You can use command-line flags to maximize the Sketchpad application window, to maximize the frontmost document window, to specify a default document for Sketchpad to open, or to specify a folder to use as the Tool Folder.

To set command-line flags, you must create a shortcut to the program itself. Windows automatically creates such a shortcut when you drag the Sketchpad icon to the Start button to install Sketchpad in the Start menu. You can also create such a shortcut on the desktop by right-clicking the Sketchpad icon and choosing **Send To | Desktop.** Consult your computer's Windows manual or online help to determine other ways to create a shortcut. Once you have created a shortcut, follow these steps to set its command-line flags.

1. If the shortcut is on the desktop, right-click the shortcut and choose **Properties.**

   If the shortcut is in the Start menu, activate the Start menu, right-click on Sketchpad, then choose **Properties.**

2. On the Shortcut panel of the Properties dialog box, click in the Target edit box and type the desired command-line flags at the end

of the existing target. Here are examples of the command-line flags you can use.

-ma Maximize the application window. The main Sketchpad window will fill your screen.

-md Maximize the first document window. When you start Sketchpad, the document window will fill the application window.

"Read Me.gsp" Open the sketch named **Read Me.gsp**.

-t "Triangle Tools" Start Sketchpad using the folder named **Triangle Tools** as the Tool Folder.

3. Click OK.

Your command-line flags will be in effect every time you run Sketchpad from the modified shortcut.

For example, if Sketchpad is installed in the folder **c:\Sketchpad**, the following target entry in the Shortcut Properties panel will start Sketchpad with the document maximized in the application window, using the folder named **My Tools** as the Tool Folder, and with the file named **Read Me.gsp** open:

```
"c:\Sketchpad\GSP 4.0.exe" -md "Read Me.gsp" -t "My Tools"
```

Advanced Tool Topics

This chapter describes advanced options available to you when creating custom tools.

Automatically Matching a Given Object

When you create a custom tool, there may be a particular given object that you would like to always match to the same object in your sketch. Normally you must match that given object each time you use the tool, even though you're matching it to the same object each time.

To save the trouble of clicking the object each time and to make the tool easier to use, you can specify that the given object should be automatically matched to the same sketch object each time the tool is used. For example, suppose you create a tool that constructs one segment on a Poincaré disk model of the hyperbolic plane. Such a tool might have three given objects: a circle defining the Poincaré disk and two points defining the segment's endpoints. Since you'd like to use the same tool repeatedly to construct multiple segments on the same Poincaré disk, it's inconvenient to have to match the given circle to the same Poincaré disk each time you use the tool. You can change your tool to automatically match this given circle to the appropriate circle in your sketch, resulting in a tool that requires you to match only two points each time you use it. Since the Poincaré disk circle is matched automatically, this tool will always create segments on the same Poincaré disk.

To match a given object automatically:

1. Open the Label Properties panel for the sketch object you want to match automatically. Assign a distinctive label to the object.

2. Choose **Show Script View** from the Custom Tools menu to show the Script View for the tool containing the given object to be matched automatically.

3. Double-click the given object in the object list to open the Properties dialog box.

4. On the Label Properties panel, assign the same label to the script object that you assigned to the sketch object.

5. Check the Automatically Match Sketch Object checkbox and close the Properties dialog box.

If all the given objects for a tool match automatically, the tool completes its construction as soon as you choose the tool. The active tool is then changed back to the **Selection Arrow** tool.

When you use the tool, it will automatically match the tool's given object to the sketch object with the same label. Provided the appropriate checkbox is checked in Label Properties, a tool containing a given point labeled "Center" will automatically match the point labeled "Center" in your sketch. If no object in the sketch has a matching label, the tool will require you to match the given object manually.

When a given object in a tool is set to match automatically, it appears in the Assuming section of the script view, rather than the Given section.

See also: Label Properties (p. 122), Script View (p. 57), Custom Tools (p. 90), Custom Tools Menu (p. 91)

Generating Specific Labels

Normally when you use a tool, the results are assigned labels just the way they would be if they were constructed normally, without using a tool. But sometimes you may want to control the labels that are used for the results of a tool. There are two types of labels you can specify when you make the tool: constant labels and variable labels.

Setting a Constant Label

A result with a constant label is assigned the same label every time the tool is used. For example, a particular line produced by a tool might always be labeled "Mirror."

To set a constant label for an object before you make the tool, use the Label Properties panel of the Properties dialog box for the sketch object that should have the constant label. Enter the desired label and check the Use Label in Custom Tools checkbox.

To set a constant label for a tool object after you make the tool, use the Custom Tools menu to show the tool's script view. Double-click the step corresponding to the resulting object that you want to have a constant label. On that object's Label Properties panel, enter the desired label and check the Use Label in Sketches checkbox.

Setting a Variable Label

When a tool has a result with a variable label, the label of the resulting object in the sketch is set based on the labels of other objects—objects that correspond to givens or other results of the tool. For instance, you can create a centroid tool that labels the centroid of a triangle based on the labels of the vertices of the triangle.

A variable label specifies how the labels of the givens and other results of the tool should be used in constructing the desired label. To specify that a particular label should be used, start the label with an equal sign (=) and enclose in curly brackets the numeric index of the object whose label should be used. The number of an object is its position in the tool's script view, starting with 1 for the first given. If a tool has three givens, the givens are numbered from 1 to 3 and the number of the first step is 4.

For example, the following variable label combines the labels of the first and second given objects of the tool:

$$= \{1\}\{2\}$$

Square brackets at the end of a label indicate that the portion of the label within square brackets should display as a subscript.

As a second example, if you create a tool to construct the centroid of a triangle, you can set the resulting centroid's label so that, if the tool is used on points A, B, and C, the centroid is labeled G_{ABC}. To accomplish this, set the centroid label in the tool to

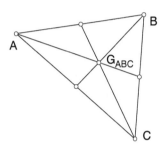

$$=G[\{1\}\{2\}\{3\}]$$

To set a variable label for a tool object, show the tool's script view using the Custom Tools menu. Double-click the step that should have the variable label to show its Properties. On the Label Properties panel, enter the desired label and check the Use Label in Sketches checkbox.

When you create a variable label for a resulting object, be sure to specify in the curly brackets only objects on which the labeled object depends. Otherwise it's possible that the labeled object will be produced before one of the objects that determines its label, and the variable label will not be created correctly.

See also: Custom Tools (p. 90), Custom Tools Menu (p. 91), Label Properties (p. 122)

Advanced Graphics Export

You can use Sketchpad to create images to paste into other programs—word processors, illustration programs, page-layout programs, and programs that create web pages. You can use Sketchpad to produce illustrations for handouts, tests, and quizzes for your class, to illustrate articles or books about geometry or algebra, or to decorate your personal web site or a web site for your class or school.

This chapter describes several useful tips and techniques that can help you produce attractive, high-quality images for such purposes.

Screen Captures

You can create a graphics file of the entire Sketchpad window, including even menus and the cursor, by using the screen capture capabilities built into Windows and Macintosh. Press the Print Screen key (Windows) or ⌘+Shift+3 (Macintosh) to take a picture of the screen. In Windows, the result is a bitmap on the clipboard; you can paste this bitmap into any program which recognizes bitmap files. On Macintosh, the result is a PICT file on the outer level of the hard drive. The first such file is named Picture 1; subsequent files are named Picture 2, Picture 3, and so forth.

Screen captures are excellent for showing what the entire screen looks like and for including a menu or the cursor in your graphic. But a screen capture does a crude job on Sketchpad graphics. Diagonal lines and circles look jagged and blocky, text is of poor quality, and resizing the image may give unexpected results.

Copying and Pasting Graphics

The clipboard graphics format in Windows is EMF (Enhanced Metafile); on Macintosh it's PICT. Most advanced graphics programs can use both formats.

You can produce high-quality images of geometric constructions using the **Copy** and **Paste** commands. For instance, you can construct a triangle in Sketchpad, select the triangle, and choose **Copy** from the Edit menu. Switch to your word processor and use **Paste** to put an image of the triangle into your word-processor document. When you use the **Copy** command, the image placed on the clipboard is not a bitmap, but encodes the actual graphics commands used to draw the object in the sketch. The resulting image displays smooth diagonal lines, circles, and text, even when scaled or when printed on a high-resolution printer.

You can even use illustration programs to edit or embellish individual components of images copied to the clipboard.

See also: Copy (p. 110)

Using Export Preferences

The Export Preferences panel has several settings you can use to obtain high-quality graphics. Hold down the Shift key and choose **Advanced Preferences** from the Edit menu to change the settings on this panel.

Improving Positioning of Objects

The graphics in this manual were copied using an export setting of 400%. After pasting they were reduced to 25% in the layout program.

Although each object is drawn smoothly, the accuracy with which copied objects are positioned remains limited by the screen resolution. When such images are scaled or printed at high resolution, visible misalignment of the objects can result. To minimize misalignment, you can set the Clipboard Image Scale to copy objects at 200%, 400%, or 800% of their normal on-screen size. When you paste the image into your word processor or graphics program, reduce it by a corresponding percentage. The result is an image with the same dimensions as the original, but with greatly increased accuracy, suitable for high-resolution printing and publication.

Arrowheads

If you want arrowheads to appear on your printed or copied image, you can check the Include Arrowheads on Lines, Rays... checkbox.

Locus Quality

When exported or printed on a high-resolution printer, the positions of the samples for point loci and functions can become visible, since the intervals between samples are drawn as segments. To produce smoother functions and loci, set the Locus/Plot Export Quality to 5x or 10x to produce either five or ten times the normal number of samples when printing or copying.

See also: Advanced Preferences (p. 138), Export Preferences (p. 138)

Cropping

Lines and rays extend far beyond the limits of the screen. Depending on the specifics of a sketch, other objects, particularly loci and function plots, may have similar extents. But when you copy such objects, you don't want an image of infinite size. Accordingly, if an image being copied extends beyond the edges of the window, Sketchpad crops the image to the window dimensions.

You can use this behavior to control the exact extent of the image copied to the clipboard. Before copying, resize and scroll your sketch window so that it shows the desired portion of the sketch. When you choose **Copy**, the clipboard image will be correctly cropped.

See also: Copy (p. 110)

PostScript and EPS Files

On both Macintosh and Windows, you can use PostScript printer drivers to produce PostScript files—files that encode the graphics to be printed in the form of a PostScript program. Such files are most commonly used for printing, either at a later time or from a different computer. But many such printer drivers also have the capability of producing EPS (Encapsulated PostScript) files, which can be placed in a wide variety of graphics programs on a wide variety of platforms.

To use your printer driver to produce an EPS file, first hide all objects in the sketch except those you want to include in the EPS file. Then choose **Print**, and use the Print dialog box to set your printer driver to produce an EPS file. The settings to produce such a file vary according to your platform and PostScript printer driver, and may not be available with all drivers. (With the Macintosh Adobe PostScript printer driver 8.7, set the Destination to File and use the PostScript settings to change the format to EPS. With certain Windows HP printer drivers, check the Print To File checkbox and use the Advanced button on Layout Properties to set the Document PostScript options to EPS.)

See also: Print (p. 108)

JavaSketchpad and Web-Based Dynamic Geometry

JavaSketchpad is a Sketchpad extension that allows you to place simple sketches inside web pages you publish on the Internet. These sketches appear as illustrations in your pages, and anyone who visits your web page can interact with them—by dragging points and pressing action buttons— directly from their web browsers, even if they don't have a copy of Sketchpad. If you create web pages, consider using

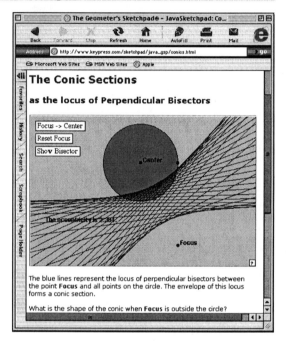

JavaSketchpad as a way to enhance any mathematics—such as personal discoveries, journal articles, class syllabi, or assignments—that you post to the web.

Not every sketch or activity you create in The Geometer's Sketchpad can be turned into an interactive JavaSketchpad illustration. Many of Sketchpad's advanced features require the full power of the program itself, rather than the slimmed-down version that visitors to your web page interact with. Also, while visitors can drag points and press action buttons in sketches you post as JavaSketchpad illustrations, they cannot draw or construct new objects. Despite these limitations, JavaSketchpad can enhance your web-publishing options significantly.

> JavaSketchpad is intentionally small in comparison to The Geometer's Sketchpad so that it downloads quickly when someone visits your web page.

Web Publishing Overview

While the full intricacies of web publishing fall beyond the scope of this book, if you've created a web page before, using JavaSketchpad should be relatively straightforward. (If you've not yet started web publishing, consider purchasing a book on the subject or searching the web itself for more information. There are thousands of sites devoted to becoming a web author.) Before getting started with JavaSketchpad, you should be familiar with these terms.

- **HTML file:** This is a document that describes the fundamental appearance of a web page and is written in HTML, the internal language of the web.

Because your browser can open local files as well as URLs, a folder on your own hard disk can serve as a web directory for JavaSketchpad testing purposes, even if it's not accessible to the general public via the Internet.

- **Web directory:** This is a storage area on your computer, or a computer you have access to, that contains HTML files that describe web pages, as well as image files and other components that appear within a web page or set of web pages that visitors can see in their browsers.

- **Applet:** This is a special computer program that resides in a web directory and that provides extended functionality to the web pages (HTML files) stored on that site. Applets are different from browser "plug-ins." Visitors have to install plug-ins to their browsers themselves, before they can access sites requiring plug-ins. In other words, plug-ins reside in the visitor's computer. Applets, on the other hand, reside in the same web directory as the HTML files that require them, so visitors don't need to worry about installing applets or reconfiguring their browsers to support them. Instead, applets are like HTML files: a visitor's browser accesses them from your web directory as needed to display your applet-enhanced web pages; the visitor doesn't have to worry about what happens "behind the scenes."

Putting this all together, JavaSketchpad is an applet that you can place in your web directory so that your HTML files present dynamic, interactive Sketchpad illustrations to your visitors.

Essential JavaSketchpad Folder Structure

Two components work behind the scenes to provide a dynamic Sketchpad illustration in a web page. The HTML file contains information that describes the geometric construction to be visualized in a language that JavaSketchpad understands. The applet—a separate set of files—provides the functionality that interprets this description, displays the figure in your visitors' browsers, and lets them interact with it. You can have many HTML files containing different illustrations that all refer to the same applet, just as on your local computer you can have many sketch documents that can all be opened by the same copy of Sketchpad.

If you can't find the JSP folder, you can reinstall it from your Sketchpad CD-ROM.

Before you create your first web page containing a construction, locate the JavaSketchpad applet itself. The applet consists of a folder titled **JSP** and the complete collection of files within that folder.

By default, when you installed Sketchpad, this folder was installed in the same directory as the Sketchpad application on your hard disk. You can copy the JSP folder from there to wherever you choose—into another folder, or onto your web server—but you should never change the contents of the folder itself. The applet only works if all of its files are in the JSP folder, with the same file and subfolder names as they had when the applet was first installed.

It's essential that you know where the JSP folder is because a web browser must be able to access the JSP folder when it displays any web page containing a Sketchpad illustration. By default, *web browers assume that the JSP folder is located in the same place as your HTML file*. Therefore, they'll only work if you store the JSP folder (or a copy of it) in the same folder as the web page itself.

Experts. If you don't want to store your HTML files in the same folder as the JSP applet, specify a relative URL from the HTML file's base directory to the JSP applet directory anywhere on your server by modifying the <CODEBASE> parameter in your HTML file. See your HTML reference manual for more details.

For example, in the following illustration, the Triangle web page has been stored in a folder (in this case, named **Web Folder**), also contains a copy of the applet folder (JSP). This is the correct relationship between web pages you create and the JSP applet that a web browser requires, whether the containing directory (in this case, Web Folder) is on your local hard disk or your web server. If you don't store the JSP folder in the same folder as your HTML file, the web browser will not be able to locate the applet and, therefore, won't display your Sketchpad illustration when you open the HTML file that describes it.

Proper folder structure (Windows and Macintosh)

Creating a JavaSketchpad Web Page

Once you've located your JSP folder, you're ready to use The Geometer's Sketchpad to create your first JavaSketchpad web page:

1. Start Sketchpad.

If this is your first time creating a JavaSketchpad illustration, start with a simple construction like a triangle.

2. Create or open a sketch containing the construction you wish to show in a web page.

3. Resize the sketch window to be the size of your intended illustration on your web page. Adjust your construction so that it appears as you'd like your visitors to first see it.

4. Choose **Save** from the File menu and save your document normally. This way you'll have a saved copy of the sketch from which you're about to create the web page.

The size of the illustration in your web page is the same as the size of your sketch window at the moment you saved the HTML file. Be sure to decrease the size of the window before saving unless you want very large web page illustrations!

5. Choose **Save As** from the File menu.

6. In the Save As dialog box, change the file format or type to **HTML/JavaSketchpad Document**.

Before saving, be sure to navigate to the folder that *contains* your JSP directory. When you're in the right place, enter an appropriate filename and click Save.

Sketchpad creates a new web page—an HTML file—describing the Sketchpad illustration.

Note: Sketchpad cannot open HTML documents, so saving your document as HTML does not save your document in a way that Sketchpad can reopen. This is the reason you did a normal save in step 4 above.

7. Assuming all goes well, Sketchpad will ask if you want to preview the web page in your browser. Click Yes.

8. Your browser opens and displays the web page. The first time your browser opens a page containing JavaSketchpad illustrations, it may take a few seconds to load.

9. Once your illustration appears, drag its independent points to explore your construction. You've successfully created your first Dynamic Geometry web page!

What Can Go Wrong

Because of the many factors involved, it may take a few tries to get things right. Here are some common JavaSketchpad mishaps and steps you can take to avoid them.

Unsupported Objects

Problem: When you save, Sketchpad warns you that not all objects were successfully saved to JavaSketchpad format.

Cause: Because JavaSketchpad is smaller than "desktop" Sketchpad, it supports fewer ways of defining objects than you can use in the desktop application. If your sketch contains objects that JavaSketchpad doesn't support, Sketchpad warns you about them—and selects the unsupported objects and their children in your sketch so that you can tell which ones were not supported. (Even when your sketch has unsupported objects, Sketchpad will save the objects that JavaSketchpad does support, so you can continue testing your web page.)

If your sketch or activity *requires* objects not supported by JavaSketchpad, you won't be able to share that sketch as an illustration. However, you can still post your original Sketchpad sketch—your .gsp file—as a downloadable file, so that visitors who use The Geometer's Sketchpad can download it and open it in Sketchpad, rather than in their browser.

To work around unsupported objects, explore different ways of constructing the same illustration. For example, at present, JavaSketchpad does not support iterations or iterated images. If your sketch contains a construction that you've iterated using the **Iterate** command, you may be able to replace it with one that you've iterated "manually" by actually constructing the first several iterations.

A complete list of objects supported by JavaSketchpad is available on the JavaSketchpad web site. Also, new versions of the applet—that support more and more Sketchpad objects—occasionally appear on the web site. See More Information (p. 233) for details.

No Preview Offered

Problem: Rather than ask whether you want to preview your file in a browser, when you save, Sketchpad warns that you saved to a folder that does not contain a copy of the JSP folder.

Cause: The HTML file must be located in the same directory as the JSP directory in order to be viewed successfully in a browser. Review the material on Essential JavaSketchpad Folder Structure (p. 227) and make sure you stored your HTML file beside your JSP folder, not inside it. Correct the situation either by moving your saved file to a folder containing the JSP applet folder or by copying the applet folder into the folder containing your saved file. Or repeat the steps described in Creating a JavaSketchpad Web Page (p. 229), choosing a different location in step 5.

Non-Java Browsers

Problem: When you preview your web page in a browser, the page contains a message reading "Sorry, this page requires a Java-capable browser."

Cause: If you have an old web browser, it may not support the Java language and, therefore, won't work with JavaSketchpad. Contact your browser manufacturer for a newer version. Alternately, it may be that your browser supports Java, but that it's currently set to disable Java applets. Go to your browser's Preferences or Options to turn on support for Java applets.

Java Exception or Error Occurs

Problem: When you preview your web page in a browser, a dialog box appears saying that a Java error or "exception" occurred.

Cause: If the message goes on to say that a "class" was not found—for example "GSP.class: class not found"—then your JSP folder is either in the wrong location or has become corrupted. (For example, vital files within it may have been accidentally deleted or moved.) Make a fresh copy of the JSP folder in the appropriate location, as described in Essential JavaSketchpad Folder Structure (p. 227).

If the error message says something else, a different problem has occurred. While JavaSketchpad has been extensively tested on current versions of Internet Explorer and Netscape Navigator, older browsers are erratic in their support of Java, and other browsers may have similar problems. (Java is a relatively new language and undergoes frequent modifications; different browsers support it to different degrees.) Check with your browser manufacturer to see if a more recent version of your browser is available. Errors or exceptions may also indicate a problem with JavaSketchpad itself. Visit the JavaSketchpad web site to see if a more recent version of the applet is available.

Appearance Discrepancies

Problem: Your sketch saves correctly and previews in your browser, but certain details in the JavaSketchpad illustration—such as choice of fonts, size of exact position of text—do not match your original sketch.

Cause: These minor discrepancies are inevitable in Java applets, where less sophisticated graphic and text services are available to an applet than to a nonapplet program (like your browser or desktop Sketchpad). What you sacrifice in appearance flexibility you gain in generality: Applets like JavaSketchpad work well on a much wider variety of computers than are capable of running the full desktop version of Sketchpad.

Modifying and Publishing Your Pages

Once you've successfully previewed a JavaSketchpad web page, you'll find that although it may be exciting to have an interactive illustration, the rest of the page is rather dull. Sketchpad adds some default text to your illustration, but otherwise leaves the page blank.

You can even put multiple JavaSketchpad illustrations on the same page by copying an <APPLET> ... </APPLET> block from one HTML file to another.

Using your favorite HTML editor, you can replace the default text and add any new HTML content to the page that you want: a description, images, links, and so forth. When editing the HTML, be careful to preserve the large <APPLET>...</APPLET> block you'll find in the middle of the page. This block describes the JavaSketchpad illustration, and the illustration may no longer function if you alter any of the contents between the <APPLET> and the </APPLET> tags.

When you're ready to share your page on the Internet, copy it and the JSP folder to your web server. Remember to keep the JSP folder in the same folder as your HTML file, even on your server. (You can store multiple HTML files in that folder and only one copy of the applet, but they must be in the same folder for JavaSketchpad to work.)

For information about other licenses, visit the JavaSketchpad web site.

Your license for The Geometer's Sketchpad includes the use of JavaSketchpad on the Internet for noncommercial purposes. The purpose of this license is to allow you to post sketches that you or your students have created using The Geometer's Sketchpad. This license is granted provided your site can be freely visited by anyone on the Internet (that is, it's not password-protected or available only to subscribers) and that no direct or indirct profit is being made by having people visit your site.

More Information

As an Internet technology, JavaSketchpad evolves rapidly, and the best source of information about it is on the web itself. The JavaSketchpad web site is the place to go for additional information; it includes sample applications, technical support, and a full description of the JavaSketchpad construction language that appears in your HTML files. You'll even find information about some features of JavaSketchpad that aren't available in The Geometer's Sketchpad.

Visit the site at

http://www.keypress.com/sketchpad/java_gsp/

Sketchpad's Internal Mathematics

Sketchpad's internal mathematics determine how the program computes and represents numbers, geometric figures, functions, and other mathematical quantities. This in turn determines how these objects appear graphically, numerically, or symbolically.

Don't confuse the *displayed* precision of a value with its internal precision or accuracy. When you display a value (such as a measurement), it appears only to the number of decimal places you choose in **Preferences** or **Properties**. Internally, that number is represented to much greater precision, as described here.

At the numeric level, Sketchpad represents point coordinates and other quantities using *64-bit floating-point arithmetic*. This standard representation for scientific computation allows your computer to represent a value with 14 to 16 significant digits of decimal precision over a wide range of magnitudes (roughly, as large as $\pm10^{300}$ and as small as $\pm10^{-300}$). While this is very precise, it is not *exact* in a mathematical sense. (For example, π cannot be represented exactly with only 15 significant digits.) Sketchpad uses tuned algorithms to attempt to represent numbers as close to their exact value as possible, and to minimize the inevitable error introduced by calculating with only a finite number of significant digits. Nonetheless, you may witness numerical error effects in the least significant digits of numbers in sketches involving a lot of internal calculation. Regrettably, no computer or computer program can represent every number exactly: there are an infinite number of numbers, of course, and—at least today!—computers have only a finite amount of memory. Thus, while Sketchpad's numeric calculations are generally reliable and can serve as the basis of a convincing argument or conjecture, a Sketchpad result should never be mistaken for constituting a mathematical proof.

At the graphical level, Sketchpad transforms its internal numeric representations into the shapes and positions that appear in your sketch window. For objects such as circles, points, and segments, the resulting images are as accurate as can be displayed on your computer screen. (When you print to a printer with higher resolution than your screen, you'll see the images are even more accurate than their on-screen representations.)

However, for plotted functions and loci, Sketchpad displays only a visual approximation of the curve's ideal mathematical shape. Primarily to maintain responsiveness when you're dragging objects, Sketchpad employs the same technique to plot these objects as a person might use if plotting them by hand: it evaluates the ideal curve at a number of different positions (called samples), then plots the curve by interpolating between these known samples. The samples themselves are very accurate, but the interpolations may or may not be, depending on the ideal shape of the mathematical object. The Plot Properties panel gives you control over how many samples Sketchpad uses to plot a function or a locus, as well as whether it displays that plot only as the (discrete) collection of accurate samples or by including the (continuous) interpolations between samples. If you consistently prefer a higher number of samples than Sketchpad uses by default, you can increase the default on the Sampling Preferences panel. Also, while Sketchpad uses approximate interpolations for display purposes, be aware that it never relies on them for mathematical purposes. Thus, if you construct a point on a function plot or on a locus (or use the Calculator to evaluate a function at given values), that point's coordinates (or function's values) are always based on the exact curve or function and not on its visual approximation.

Finally, at the symbolic level, Sketchpad performs simple computer algebra to differentiate functions when you use the **Derivative** command from the Graph menu. While these computed derivatives are generally reliable for graphing and evaluation purposes, they may not be exact. In particular, when differentiating intricate functions, Sketchpad may fail to simplify the result fully, introducing point discontinuities in the derivative; and Sketchpad does not compute domain restrictions on the derivative function. Use **Derivative** to compute the slope of a function at an arbitrary point for graphing purposes or for mathematical constructions, but be sure to verify the result before using it as the basis of a mathematical proof.

See also: Accuracy vs. Precision (p. 136), Plot Properties (p. 124), Sampling Preferences (p. 139), Derivative (p. 203), Unit Preferences (p. 135)

Index

The Geometer's Sketchpad Reference Manual

The Geometer's Sketchpad Reference Manual

The Geometer's Sketchpad Reference Manual

URL
  linking to, 114, 132
Value Properties, 123
Values, 20, 49
  See also Measurements;
    Calculations; Parameters
  display name, 123
  precision, 135
  units, 135
  using in calculations, 20, 52
  using to set color, 145
  using to set iterative depth, 185
  using to transform objects, 167,
    168, 170

Variable labels in custom tools,
  221
Vertical lines, 85
Visibility of objects, 9
Window border, 6
Window list, 205
Window menu, 205
World Wide Web (WWW)
  export, 226–33
  linking to, 114, 132
Zoom, 76
Zoom box, 6